NARCISSUS

FROM

RUBBLE

NARCISSUS *from* RUBBLE

COMPETING MODELS OF CHARACTER IN CONTEMPORARY BRITISH AND AMERICAN FICTION

Julius Rowan Raper

Louisiana State University Press Baton Rouge and London

Manufactured in the United States of America
First printing
01 00 99 98 97 96 95 94 93 92 5 4 3 2 1

Designer: Rebecca Lemna
Typeface: Galliard
Typesetter: Graphic Composition, Inc.
Printer and binder: Thomson-Shore, Inc.

LIBRARY OF CONGRESS CATALOGING-IN-PUBLICATION DATA:
Raper, Julius Rowan, 1938–
Narcissus from rubble : competing models of character in contemporary British and American fiction / Julius Rowan Raper.
p. cm.
Includes bibliographical references and index.
ISBN 0-8071-1712-9 (alk. paper)
1. American fiction—20th century—History and criticism.
2. English fiction—20th century—History and criticism.
3. Characters and characteristics in literature. 4. Narcissism in literature. 5. Self in literature. I. Title.
PS374.C43R37 1992
823′.9109384—dc20 91-32604
CIP

The author is grateful to the editors of the following journals for permission to use material from his previously published articles that have appeared under these titles: "Running Contrary Ways: Saul Bellow's *Seize the Day,*" *Southern Humanities Review,* X (Spring, 1976), 157–68; "John Fowles: The Psychological Complexity of *The Magus,*" *American Imago,* XLV (Spring, 1988), 61–84; "John Barth's *Chimera:* Men and Women Under the Myth," *Southern Literary Journal,* XXII (Fall, 1989), 17–31; "The Philosopher's Stone and Lawrence Durrell's Psychological Vision in *Monsieur* and *Livia,*" *Twentieth Century Literature,* XXXVI (Winter, 1991), 419–33.

The paper in this book meets the guidelines for permanence and durability of the Committee on Production Guidelines for Book Longevity of the Council on Library Resources.♾

Thanks to the large-spirited:

family, students, friends

BEARINGS

N: And still deeper the meaning of that story of Narcissus . . .
this is the key to it all.

—Herman Melville, *Moby-Dick*

S: We don't see things as they are. We see them as we are.

—Traditional wisdom

W: And if the Wise Man's Stone were found,
The stone would lack the wise man still.

—Goethe, *Faust,* II, 5063–64
Charles E. Passage translation

E: The mark of a moderate man
is freedom from his own ideas.

—Lao-tzu, *Tao Te Ching*
Stephen Mitchell translation

Contents

PREFACE

The Transcenders

When we look for predecessors of protagonists in contemporary fiction, we may go back to a young man who, when told to kill his uncle the king, hesitated. Or we may turn to a whaling captain who elected to say no to the sailing master of a universe that horribly scarred and maimed him. We may even look back to Prometheus, who defied the ruler of the gods on behalf of the lowly race of men, or to Achilleus, who passionately refused to act as his king required. Moving closer to our own era, we may think of any number of black men, named and unnamed, who rejected the roles society thrust on them: a runaway slave who called a white boy "Trash"; a musician who elected to become an Ex-Colored Man; a chauffeur who refused to accept his identity from a racist society, from his millionaire employers, or from his Marxist lawyer.

In all cases, these forerunners of modern heroes were driven to "self"-transcendence—to rejecting the self that their culture offered them. They said no to an identity that seemed built into the nature of things, one as old as time itself. In the language of John Fowles, they came to know exactly what they hated, and they fought to put it behind them for all time.

But in saying no to one role, they inadvertently said yes to another. Hamlet became a half-sane hesitater, Ahab, the mad destroyer of his crew, Prometheus, a bound god, Achilleus, the murderer of his best friend, Jim, a recaptured slave, and Bigger Thomas, an executed murderer. Even James Weldon Johnson's Ex-Colored Man ends with regrets and guilt for deserting the cause of his race. Again in Fowles's words, the predecessors of our heroes found where they hated, but they did not find where they loved. They became heroes of role transcendence, but in the process they embraced a role poorly connected to the core of their being.

Like the powerful and complex philosophy that our century has developed to explain its intellectual heroes, these characters believed for a time that the heady freedom of transcendence was the very purpose of their existence. Theirs was a sensation of freedom so exhilarating that striving toward it seemed worth all costs, including denial of the biological ground of freedom itself. All who work with the novels of Herman Melville, Richard Wright, Ralph Ellison, William Styron, and Norman Mailer have, time and time again, encountered this ecstatic transcendence, often in a context of creative violence. It is the freedom that Jean-Paul Sartre so eloquently defends in his major philosophical works. At times, it may seem the culmination of the human enterprise that begins when we defy gravity and biology, our physical and genetic heritages, by standing upright and fixing our eyes, not on the ground, but on the transcendent world of ideas, spirit, stars. One can hardly question the nobility of this endeavor or number the centuries during which it provided the central motive of human life.

There has, however, been a cost. We may have reached the acme of the enterprise toward transcendence. That, at least, seems to be the warning, sometimes implicit, often explicit, in the eleven contemporary novels on which the study that follows focuses. For these novels suggest that sometime between 1900 and 1945 we reached the point where we should have turned back to reestablish our ties with human biology and the natural world. We did not, or only a few did. Because we did not, the Jeremiahs of our generation tell us, we have persisted in a conspiracy to destroy ourselves.

The program of self-annihilation dramatized in this group of novels includes the terrible products of our technology that each of us may think of immediately. But the conspiracy goes deeper and takes more pernicious, less visible, forms. It haunts even our best-intended attempts to improve our lot: our arts, our entertainment, our seemingly innocuous commercial products, our ideologies—our philosophy itself.

These six novelists are not mere doom-singing television evangelists. The solutions that Saul Bellow, Thomas Pynchon, Jerzy Kosinski, Fowles, John Barth, and Lawrence Durrell offer are more demanding than a simple return to the traditions and gods of our fathers. The advice of the Delphic oracle comes closer: *gnothi seauton,* "know thyself." However difficult that mandate was for ancient Greeks to obey, there is today, as our oracles show, considerably more self to know.

Knowing oneself is not without its own risk, one most often associated with what Sigmund Freud called narcissism, the focusing of mental energy chiefly on the ego. Narcissism is an orientation that Durrell explored with great originality in his series of influential, experimental novels, *The Alexandria Quartet,* published from 1957 to 1960. Eventually, though, he and the other authors discussed here worked their way through the maze that Freud termed narcissism, as well as through the hazards of self-transcendence, and, like the revisionist psychoanalyst Heinz Kohut, arrived at an understanding of narcissism less judgmental and more perceptive than Freud's earlier formulation.

In the struggle, first to comprehend the dangers of the self-transcending tendencies of our culture and then to become completely what we are beyond our roles, lies the drama on which these authors and this study focus.

I wish to express my appreciation to the Institute for the Arts and the Humanities, University of North Carolina, in which I was a fellow during the summer of 1988, and to the University of North Carolina Department of English for an Individual Study Assignment during the spring semester, 1990.

ABBREVIATIONS

AS — Heinz Kohut. *The Analysis of the Self.* New York, 1971.

HDAC — Heinz Kohut. *How Does Analysis Cure?* Edited by Arnold Goldberg. Chicago, 1984.

LV — Lawrence Durrell. *Livia, or Buried Alive.* New York, 1984.

Ma — John Fowles. *The Magus.* Boston, 1965.

Mr — Lawrence Durrell. *Monsieur.* New York, 1984.

RS — Heinz Kohut. *The Restoration of the Self.* New York, 1977.

TE — C. G. Jung. *Two Essays on Analytical Psychology.* Translated by R. F. C. Hull. New York, 1956.

NARCISSUS
FROM
RUBBLE

INTRODUCTION

The Pull of Proteus

In 1900 two books appeared in German that, though sharply opposed to one another, were to shape much of the intellectual and literary landscape of the twentieth century. Each work marked the beginning of a major current of modern thought, for each was the first important book by a thinker whose bold new perspective would inspire hundreds of studies by loyal disciples and earnest dissenters. The books I have in mind are *Logical Investigations,* by German philosopher Edmund Husserl, and *The Interpretation of Dreams,* by Austrian psychologist Sigmund Freud; the intellectual currents that flowed from their pens are modern phenomenology and psychoanalysis. By the final decade of the century, each current had spread across the intellectual landscape, but the focus of this study falls on ways each influenced the novel in England and America during the second half of the century.

It may well be that novelists intend to write from real life, to give their readers a faithful account of people and places they have observed and recorded. It may also be, as economists of literature say, that material conditions govern human behavior. But in contemporary literature, ideas about behavior have played a vital part. This study demonstrates that two powerful ideas, two competing models of the mind, have done much to determine what specific material conditions novelists, and the characters in their books, have allowed to control the characters' behavior. It also shows that these very different ways of viewing the self have governed the fashion in which fictional characters have elected to relate themselves to material reality. Following one model, that of Husserl, they have chosen to adapt themselves to the external world. Following the other, attributed to Freud, they have used objects in the outer world for their own purposes: to know themselves in the multiple aspects of their being. Thus phrased, the thesis of this study is simple to comprehend.

What makes the task here difficult is that the two models I have in mind—the phenomenological model associated with existentialism and the psychological model after Freud—not only have passed through numberless variations in fiction but have grown out of and have governed much of the intellectual ferment of our century. The fields they have shaped vary from philosophy and psychology (with which the models are immediately associated) to economics, anthropology, politics, theology, and literary criticism. In order to focus on a manageable topic, I must restrict this investigation to two of these disciplines, philosophy and psychology, and, in turn, narrow the span of attention to ways they affect characterization in contemporary fiction. I have had to limit variations in the two models further to those that my knowledge of the eleven novels under consideration suggests have most influenced the novelists, that is, to variations that most enrich our comprehension of the fictions. For the phenomenological model, I have drawn primarily on theories of Husserl and Jean-Paul Sartre, with some references to Martin Heidegger. For the psychological model, I have most frequently used the variations developed by Carl G. Jung and Heinz Kohut but have drawn on Freud where his formulations have greater explanatory power.

In short, my approach is eclectic, and my knowledge far from universal. For many years I lived and thought from the phenomenological perspective, but the present study, for reasons it demonstrates, comes down firmly on the psychological side of the dispute. Knowing where I stand may help readers evaluate my response to the rich, inexhaustible books under discussion. In this way we can free ourselves from misunderstandings in a field of study where differing points of view surely exist and should, I think, continue to do so. I wish to persuade, not to impose my present position on people kind enough to read what I write.

Not every thinker believes, as I do, that the two models are opposed to one another. For example, since 1970 a school of thought called phenomenological psychology has published the *Journal of Phenomenological Psychology*. Beyond the broad policy and purpose announced by its editors in the premiere issue, it is difficult to understand exactly how such a school came into being, for the issues that distinguish modern phenomenology from psychoanalysis as their founders envisioned them are essential ones. Freud, working in the Darwinian tradition, focused on a biologically grounded psyche, much of which necessarily remains unconscious. Husserl, in contrast, working from Cartesian assumptions, strove to free a pure transcendental consciousness from the determinants of biology and psychology. To the degree that phenomenological psychology privileges Husserl's pure consciousness, it cannot honor Freud's greatest discovery, the force of the unconscious mind. To the degree, however, that phenomenological psychology works with the "bracketed" materials that "contaminate" an otherwise pure consciousness, the school may contribute to an understanding of personality and character. (The discussion of Herbert Stencil in Thomas Pynchon's *V.* that follows demonstrates one way psychological problems may arise after phenomenological bracketing.) Nonetheless, in seeking pure consciousness, phenomenology places its values, from the psychoanalytical perspective, in the wrong place.

Arguments about pure consciousness and biological grounding appear theoretical and abstract, but the effects of choosing one position over the other can be very practical. For example, we may not take our popular culture seriously when it says that we are what we eat. We do listen, though, when psychoanalysis suggests that we are what we dream. Both authorities assert a biological ground for personality. In bold contrast, the philosophy of our century tells us that we are our consciousness of objects. This is a simple claim, but a world of meaning lies back of it. And, if contemporary novelists are correct, a world of danger.

The possibility that we are our consciousness of objects goes back to a split occurring in 1900. I speak of the division between logic and psychology that takes place in Husserl's *Logical Investigations*—a division that first entered the English literary world in essays by T. E. Hulme that shaped the main current of modernist writing. Husserl's logic, which became the foundation of phenomenology, also exerted a major influence on Sartre, among many others. Sartre's elaborate exposition of existentialism, in turn, inspired much of the most original European and American writing after World War II.

Although the year 1900 also saw publication of Freud's key work, the appearance of *The Interpretation of Dreams* was an event that Husserl's followers were destined to ignore or play down, given their resistance to psychology and their commitment to a transcendental ego free of natural, and therefore psychological, definitions. Freud and his followers made possible much powerful twentieth-century writing, too, and as one would expect, this writing differs from that inspired by phenomenology.

Although this split between Husserl and Freud, between phenomenology and psychoanalysis as the two perspectives influence British and American fiction since 1960 or so, is the subject of the present essay, the study is not, for the most part, a venture into abstract philosophy or metapsychology. In fiction, the division I speak of here expresses itself in very concrete forms. It significantly affected the kinds of characters novelists developing from each of the currents found it possible to create. It is on the characters, their backgrounds in the thought of our century, and their effects on readers that I focus in the pages that follow. Some of the novels examined take only one of the two streams as their central concern. Others dramatize the implicit conflict between the two approaches to character. Occasionally a work conceived in one perspective means something very different, yet significant, if interpreted from the other. In all cases, keeping the differences between the two outlooks clearly in mind expands the meaning of the text under consideration.

From the perspective of modern philosophy, the claim that we are our consciousness of objects rests on a tradition that goes back to René Descartes. For modern philosophy begins with the blurring of epistemology and ontology, knowledge and being, what we know and what we are—a blurring found in Descartes' famous assumption, "I think; therefore I am."

Descartes was not the first philosopher to equate knowledge and being. At the beginnings of Western philosophy, the Pre-Socratics honored matter. Thales had his water, Heraclitus, the fire, Empedocles, the four elements, Democritus, the atoms. Plato, however, offered ideas as true being. With Plato before them, philosophers were quick to see where their interests lay, and, no doubt in part because Plato gave thinkers more comfort than did his predecessors, the propositions he put forth became those to which Western philosophers have, for good or ill, so often provided the footnotes. After Plato, knowing and being were, all too often, indiscriminately mixed.

Although Charles Darwin's discoveries helped undermine Plato's assumption about the priority of ideas relative to things, the twentieth century did not escape the Platonic mix. If the century began with Western thought much under Darwin's influence, with natural history and instinctive models of human behavior in the ascendency, this was a dominance of body over mind that twentieth-century intellectuals did not allow to persist. From the start, Husserl in *Logical Investigations* worked diligently, as Michael H. Levenson's *A Genealogy of Modernism* shows, to cleanse logic of the taint of a psychological (and therefore natural) grounding.

Husserl, according to Levenson, "speaks with scorn of 'our psychologically obsessed age'" and bitterly contests J. S. Mill's contention that logic itself takes its theoretical grounds wholly from psychology. In laying the groundwork for modern phenomenology, Husserl asserts that logic "borrows nothing from anything"; rather, "it is pure, ideal and objective." Husserl's need to liberate logic from material foundations would lead him to posit the existence of the pure "transcendental ego" as that which "we truly are without knowing it." We become this transcendental ego only through an "ascetic attitude of detachment," only by suspending judgment "concerning the world, things in the world, even our own feelings, emotions, and inner psychological life."[1] In short, such logical purity carries a distinct cost.

It is a cost, however, that modernist thinkers and artists were ready to pay. Levenson goes on to describe how eagerly Hulme, Ezra Pound's model Imagist poet and theoretician of the Imagist aesthetic, embraced Husserl's phenomenological view of logic as a way to get rid of the anthropomorphism that Hulme believed threatened to swamp logic, mathematics, ethics, and other intellectual endeavors in a subjectivity that had no validity beyond reference to the human mind. At this point in his development, Hulme wished to slough off the personal, subjective, and psychological currents that earlier dominated his own aesthetics and the aesthetics of his contemporaries. What drew him to Husserl was the philosopher's desire to free logic from its psychological grounding and to demonstrate that modern philosophy, in imitation of modern science, could be based instead on pure, ideal, and objective consciousness of objects. Husserl provided the escape

1. Michael H. Levenson, *A Genealogy of Modernism: A Study of English Literary Doctrine, 1908–1922* (Cambridge, Eng., 1986), 91; James M. Edie, "Introduction," in Gaston Berger, *The "Cogito" in Husserl's Philosophy,* trans. Kathleen McLaughlin (Evanston, Ill., 1972), xx.

Hulme sought "from the confines of the human personality"; Husserl's objectivity allowed Hulme to "purge the last vestiges of humanism from his thought," to "insist that questions of ultimate value had nothing to do with subjectivity."[2]

Hulme's search for pure objective knowledge included an aesthetic dimension that came to dominate much of the art of our century. It was probably during his 1912 trip from London to Berlin, according to Levenson, that Hulme came across the work of Husserl and certainly then that he encountered *Abstraktion und Einfühlung,* or *Abstraction and Empathy: A Contribution to the Psychology of Style,* published in 1908 by Wilhelm Worringer. Worringer's influential doctoral dissertation argues that the Western aesthetic, going back to the classical Greeks and especially since the Renaissance, has been dominated by empathy, the sense that the beauty of objects resides in the freedom they give me (in the language of Theodor Lipps) to "live myself out in them." For Worringer, "the urge to empathy . . . finds its gratification in the beauty of the organic," in what the object shares with the observer. Empathy as the volition of art arises from "a happy pantheistic relationship of confidence between man and the phenomena of the external world."[3]

What attracted Hulme, however, and what would shape the modernist aesthetic, was Worringer's assertion that beauty may also be created from an urge that runs counter to empathy, the urge to abstraction, the sense that beauty resides "in the life-denying inorganic, in the crystalline or, in general terms, in all abstract law and necessity." Worringer finds the urge to abstraction in the pyramids, Byzantine mosaics, primitive epochs of art, Oriental art, and especially geometric styles. In passages that illuminate the aesthetics of subsequent modernists, especially T. S. Eliot and Pound, he contends that "the urge to abstraction is the outcome of a great inner unrest inspired in man by the phenomena of the outside world." Like the transcendental tinge in religions, it arises from "an immense spiritual dread of space"—the dread and fear that drove the Eastern mind toward whatever promised tranquillity above the relativity of Maya. Primitive cultures especially need abstraction, to compensate for the flux, to remove them from the

2. Levenson, *Genealogy of Modernism,* 91–93.

3. *Ibid.,* 94; Wilhelm Worringer, *Abstraction and Empathy: A Contribution to the Psychology of Style,* trans. Michael Bullock (New York, 1953), 4, 7, 15.

forces of nature, to escape the tormenting entanglement of "interrelationship and flux" caused by the "phenomena of the outer world." Abstraction offers happiness not in projecting the self into things but in placing things of the external world outside arbitrariness, thus finding in the beauty created a "refuge from appearances."[4]

It requires little imagination to detect parallels between Husserl's idea of the transcendental ego and the abstract urge to escape the ever-changing phenomena of the external world. Nor is it difficult to find parallels between Worringer's division between empathy and abstraction, on the one hand, and key events in modernist writing, on the other. For example, Eliot's *The Waste Land* reflects as keenly as any Byzantine mosaic a spiritual dread of the world of change, appearances, and entanglement, and the quest in his *Four Quartets* for the still point of the turning world represents the desire to escape the flux and entanglement of the forces of nature. In a different manner, the surface naturalism of James Joyce's *Ulysses* captures the world of particularity and flux as forcefully as any literary work ever has, while the familiar mythic parallels that give the novel its name betray the author's urge to move his Dublin toward abstraction and thus rescue it from arbitrariness.

The parallel influences of an abstract aesthetic and of Husserl's transcendental logic have thus existed in modernist writing since Hulme went to Berlin; that is, they have been there from the beginning. But World War II was a turning point in modern art and literature as well as in modern politics. After the war, the major European influences flowed from France, not Germany. France provided Albert Camus, Simone de Beauvoir, Maurice Merleau-Ponty, Sartre, and, more recently, Alain Robbe-Grillet, Michel Butor, Nathalie Sarraute, Claude Simon, Jacques Lacan, and many others. Larger than anyone else loomed Sartre—Sartre, too, was France. Even so, behind Sartre stood the German thinkers Husserl and Husserl's student Martin Heidegger. Husserl's struggle against the intrusion of psychology into philosophy determined the background of Heidegger's own doctoral dissertation, completed at Freiburg in 1914. It is on Husserl, therefore, that we must focus in discussing Sartre here.

From Husserl, Sartre borrowed the idea of intentionality, the notion that consciousness is a pure "directedness toward objects," that

4. Worringer, *Abstraction and Empathy*, 4, 14–18, 20.

"consciousness is essentially a directedness toward what it is not," that it " 'has objects' which are always outside of and independent of itself." Husserl's position continues: "This experience of not being one's objects, of not even *being* oneself, this ability to always take a distance from any object, and to objectify and articulate any situation, is the most fundamental root of the experience of freedom. It is the basis of the very phenomenological proof of being free."[5] In his *Nachwort,* he had asserted, "I . . . *am the 'transcendental ego,'*" meaning "I myself as this individual essence, posited absolutely, as the open infinite field of pure phenomenological data and their inseparable unity."[6] Husserl set out to create a more perfect epistemology, but before he stopped, he had also generated an ontology, a theory of being.

Between 1911 and 1913, and again in the 1920s, Husserl tried to "bridge the gap between empirical [biological, naturalistic] psychology and transcendental phenomenology with help of a completely new science" that he eventually called "phenomenological psychology." The goal of this endeavor was to obtain knowledge of the purely psychical, from which all "physical and psychophysical experience" was eliminated. Knowledge of the purely psychical also required eliminating all prejudices borrowed from other sciences, from tradition, and from traditional logic. Phenomenological psychology had, furthermore, to omit external experience by bracketing the "real world." Husserl's intent was to bring this purified psychology as close as possible to his transcendental phenomenology.[7]

Since Husserl, phenomenological psychology has split into two camps. The members of one group seek an accommodation between empirical psychology and phenomenological philosophy. They speak of only "*a school or trend* within" empirical psychology, one grounded in phenomenological philosophy. The second group follow Husserl more closely by claiming "that phenomenological psychology provides empirical psychology with the necessary foundation" for its research, descriptions, and interpretations. This second group is more

5. James M. Edie, *Edmund Husserl's Phenomenology* (Bloomington, 1987), 67.

6. Quoted *ibid.,* 71.

7. Joseph J. Kockelmans, "Husserl's Original View on Phenomenological Psychology," in *Phenomenological Psychology: The Dutch School,* ed. Joseph J. Kockelmans (Dordrecht, The Netherlands, 1987), 5–6, 14–16, 19, 22.

philosophical than biological. Its influence, in general and especially on literature, has been significant because its most important exponent was Sartre.[8]

Building on Husserl's phenomenological ontology, Sartre, in *The Transcendence of the Ego,* written in 1936 and 1937, raised consciousness one step higher, purified it one degree more than Descartes and Husserl, by arguing that "I am consciousness of" whatever object, physical or mental, present or imagined, my intention fixes upon. More accurately, Sartre said, "there is consciousness of this chair" or of this object or that object, and if I reflect on this consciousness, I discover the *I* as the transcendent object of my reflective act.[9] From Sartre's proposition that the *I* freely becomes consciousness of whatever object it attends to, a great deal follows. There is Sartre's own phenomenological ontology, his brilliant exposition of the consequences of being nothing but "consciousness of" an object, as set forth in the six hundred pages of *Being and Nothingness,* which appeared in 1943. In later French literature this freedom to become objects of consciousness leads to the thinginess or object-ridden texture of the French New Novel, especially as created by Robbe-Grillet in *Le Voyeur, La Jalousie, La Maison de Rendezvous,* and other works. Sartre's position also significantly affected American fiction and criticism.

In 1946 or 1947, Richard Wright met Sartre in the United States and began reading his works as well as those of Albert Camus. The excitement of this reading was so intense that he told a friend, "They are writing of things that I have been thinking, writing and feeling all of my life." Because Wright valued Sartre's perspective, existential readings of Wright's earlier work, especially *Native Son,* published in 1940, carry an implied stamp of authorial approval, despite Wright's qualifying remark that what he wrote was "fact not philosophy." Wright's demurral itself implies that critics since 1946 or 1947 might also be on the right track in looking to earlier black authors for existential elements if they, too, wrote from the facts of their own experience. A black man in a white culture lives daily the basic existential drama of saying no to what the culture tells him he is in order to say yes to what

8. *Ibid.,* 28.

9. Jean-Paul Sartre, *The Transcendence of the Ego: An Existentialist Theory of Consciousness,* trans. Forrest Williams and Robert Kirkpatrick (New York, 1957), 53–54.

he thinks he can be. The tragic-mulatto stories of Charles Chesnutt and Jean Toomer raise the existential questions of identity as surely as does William Faulkner's novel about Joe Christmas, *Light in August,* published in 1932, and Faulkner's great story is one of the authorities Sartre cites in his major philosophical work, *Being and Nothingness.*[10] In effect, American novelists, black and white, for the list would have to include Herman Melville, James Weldon Johnson, and Ernest Hemingway, were, in some ways, existentialists before Sartre and Camus made the philosophy a major movement during the middle third of the twentieth century.

My purpose here, however, is not to argue the sources of existentialism, even in the English-speaking world. It is to establish that an awareness of the existential perspective existed among English-speaking writers even before Ralph Ellison published *Invisible Man* in 1952, Iris Murdoch, her philosophical study *Sartre, Romantic Rationalist* in 1953, and Wright, his self-consciously existential novel *The Outsider,* also in 1953. We may detect deliberate existential elements even as early as Saul Bellow's *The Dangling Man* in 1944, a possibility much debated by critics of Bellow.[11] In any case, by 1956, when Bellow published *Seize the Day,* the earliest of the eleven novels discussed in the present study, the existential outlook was an important current in Anglo-American literary circles, one strong enough to provoke the sort of challenge to its view of the human situation found in *Seize the Day* and the novels that follow.

In addition to the parallels between Sartre's position and the dilemma faced by Wright and other black American authors, and more central to the subject of this study, modern phenomenological thought generates a remarkable type of character, recognizable as early as the enigmatic Rinehart of Ellison's *Invisible Man,* and accurately identified in Robert J. Lifton's important essay "Protean Man," which came out in 1968. According to Lifton, Protean man continuously re-creates his self (taken as an individual's symbol of his or her own organism). In offering Sartre's life and work as an example of the Protean style, Lif-

10. Constance Webb, *Richard Wright: A Biography* (New York, 1968), 279, 281; Jean-Paul Sartre, *Being and Nothingness: An Essay on Phenomenological Ontology* (New York, 1956), 405–406.

11. See Ada Aharoni, "Bellow and Existentialism," *Saul Bellow Journal,* II (1983), 42–54, and Robert Alter, "The Stature of Saul Bellow," *Midstream,* X (December, 1964), 3–15.

ton quotes Theodore Solotaroff's statement of Sartre's fundamental assumption: "There is no such thing as even a relatively fixed sense of self, ego or identity—rather, there is only the subjective mind in motion in relationship to that which it confronts." Lifton offers numerous examples of Protean figures in America, including characters in books by Bellow, Jack Kerouac, and John Barth, as well as the style of composer John Cage.[12] For Sartre's concept of freedom as an open field of becoming strikes a very deep and ancient chord in the American psyche, the cherished sense that Americans have always been free to become New Men simply by pressing westward into the New Eden.

For Lifton, "this Protean style is by no means pathological." Indeed, it "may be one of the functional patterns necessary to life in our times."[13] In our history, the sense of open possibilities has proven one of the positive tenets of the American myth. If Bellow and Pynchon are right, however, the desire to change as freely as the Old Man of the Sea is not without risks.

12. Robert Jay Lifton, *Boundaries: Psychological Man in Revolution* (New York, 1970), 38, 46, 49, 51.

13. *Ibid.*, 44.

1 The Limits of Change: Saul Bellow's *Seize the Day* and *Henderson the Rain King*

RUNNING CONTRARY WAYS

Saul Bellow's fourth and fifth novels, *Seize the Day* and *Henderson the Rain King,* published in 1956 and 1959, respectively, approach the drama that is our subject from a perspective both complex and ambivalent. The major actor in the first, Tommy Wilhelm, needs desperately to change. But Wilhelm has already attempted all the Protean variations he can imagine, and they have left him at his wits' end, seeking an older, wiser man who will tell him what to do with his life. He has no sense of the inner resources he possesses to fall back on.

The protagonist of the other novel, Eugene H. Henderson, is hardly as desperate as Wilhelm, but he, too, desires to transform his life. His relative freedom from despair and his eagerness to accommodate the people he encounters make him an ideal candidate for change. Indeed, there is much talk in *Henderson the Rain King* about personal transformation, so much that readers may be tempted to see the novel as a portrait of Protean variability. The changes through which Henderson passes, however, are more complex than mere alterations in the objects of his consciousness.

Although Bellow's two novels dramatize characters who vary the objects on which they focus, the books finally do not propose that contemporary man can develop by simply changing the objects that interest him. The two fictions direct attention instead toward the resources the characters have within themselves to enable them to oppose the abstractly objective forces working against the individual in cultures as different as New York City and tribal Africa. Both novels, like the body of Bellow's work, challenge that predilection of modernism championing abstraction and objectivity rather than empathy and subjectivity.

Bellow's first novel, *The Dangling Man,* published in 1944, opens with spirited promises to eschew the hardboiled pose dominant in American life and literature and to end the tradition of "closemouthed straightforwardness" that runs, he implies, from Rudyard Kipling through Hemingway to the literary offspring of Hemingway. For this tradition, he wishes to substitute a confessional literature that feels no shame in being introspective and self-indulgent or in talking about feelings, emotions, and the inner life. Among the other memorable passages of the first novel are conversations the protagonist Joseph carries on with the Spirit of Alternatives, an alter-personality that emerges to guide him beyond the position his reason guards to where he might discover his "inmost feelings."

In one form or another, the Spirit of Alternatives appears in six of the book-length works by Bellow. It makes its presence felt in the irrational attraction that pulls Leventhal toward Allbee the anti-Semite of *The Victim,* published in 1947, destitute Tommy Wilhelm toward Tamkin the confidence man of *Seize the Day,* and introverted Arthur Sammler toward the elegantly dressed black pickpocket in *Mr. Sammler's Planet,* which came out in 1969. The Spirit of Alternatives also haunts Henderson as he exchanges roles with King Dahfu in *Henderson the Rain King* and Bummidge the comedian when he madly wills to become Bummidge the Freudian intellectual in *The Last Analysis,* which appeared in 1964.

These variations in the Spirit of Alternatives and their hold on the protagonists of these works reflect Bellow's belief that the conventional novel of the "unitary personality" offers little more than narcotic entertainment for an age that has grown used to discovering "dubious selves" within each of us. The old personality defended with "grace under pressure" by writers of the hardboiled school is viewed more and more as the "presentation self," the persona one improvises to play the limited roles required by society. The real self remains "unknown . . . hidden, a sunken power in us," perhaps only " a quaintly organized chaos of instinct and spirit." The true identity, if there is one, "lies deep—very deep."[1] In Bellow's concern with the persona, the real self, and the Spirit of Alternatives, the influence of psychoanalysis, especially the Jungian school, appears central, though critics more commonly mention Wilhelm Reich.[2] While Reichian "character armor" closely parallels the Jungian persona, the Jungian libido and the Real Self are concepts of greater complexity than Reich's "full orgastic potency." Jungian theory contains nuances useful for discussing Bellow's notion of an alternative self.

Of Bellow's six variations on the theme that a man's character develops by running contrary ways, none has as broad and immediate application to American society as the change in Tommy Wilhelm's personality in *Seize the Day,* a novel thought by many, despite its meager size, to be one of Bellow's finest achievements. Here Bellow seems to have discovered a structure unusual, if not unique, in the impact achieved by what it leaves out. From the start, he points every incident toward the final scene. The book opens with Tommy Wilhelm descending an elevator, very much afraid that he is in for a major crisis; the second paragraph ends with his awareness that "his routine [is] about to break up" and that "a huge trouble long presaged but till now formless" will have to be faced before evening.[3] From time to time thereafter, Tommy reminds us that this is to be his "day of reckoning," that he stands at the edge of a crisis. Often he experiences the confusion and anguish associated with the threshold of conversions, a possibility he seems to sense when at the end of the first chapter he prays: "Let me out of this clutch and into a different life. For I am all balled up. Have mercy" (26). Then, in the final scene, standing by the coffin of a total stranger and drowning in his own tears, he sinks "deeper than sorrow . . . toward the consummation of his heart's ultimate

1. Saul Bellow, "Where Do We Go from Here: The Future of Fiction," in *The Theory of the American Novel,* ed. George Perkins (New York, 1970), 443–45.

2. Helge Normann Nilson, in "Saul Bellow and Wilhelm Reich," *American Studies in Scandinavia,* X (1978), 81–91, and Eusebio L. Rodrigues, in "Reichianism in *Henderson the Rain King,*" *Criticism,* XV (1973), 212–33, discuss the influence of Wilhelm Reich on Bellow.

3. Saul Bellow, *Seize the Day* (New York, 1961), 4; hereinafter cited parenthetically by page number in the text.

need" (118). This is a puzzling ending, for it leaves dangling any reader habituated to the traditional dramatic rhythm of purpose-passion-perception. Where is the perception phase, the clarification?

The novel gives a strong sense of preparation and struggle, building up to the climax at the stranger's funeral, but just when one expects the falling action to unravel and explain, the book ends. What this truncation of the action accomplishes is the close identification of the reader with the initially unappealing Tommy, who remains a loser while all about him men are making fortunes in a rising market. At the end, the reader stands very much where Tommy stands, with a more or less profound emotional catharsis on his hands, wondering why this crying jag should be part of "the consummation of [Tommy's] heart's ultimate need." The answer to this question, had Bellow chosen to spell it out, would have constituted the perception phase of the novel. The solution, however, is implicit if we correctly answer a preliminary question: what is wrong with Tommy that he should feel he is headed for a breakdown?

In his middle forties, Tommy Wilhelm finds himself out of work, separated (but not divorced) from his wife and two sons, and living again with his father, or at least in the same building, the Gloriana, a swanky retirement hotel on upper Broadway. Down to his last seven hundred dollars and with little prospect of a new position, he faces a future of endless payments of support money. Worse yet, his father, a wealthy and affable old gentleman named Dr. Adler, time and again refuses, on principle, to help his hopeless son out; the old man, who has settled down to long years of healthy old age surrounded by admiring contemporaries in the Gloriana, will tolerate none of Tommy's begging for money, advice, and sympathy. All he offers is a contemptuous "I warned you!" Despite these rejections, Tommy says, and believes, when asked whether he loves his old man: "Of course, of course I love him. My father. My mother—" (92). Obviously he has never given the matter much thought; fathers are simply the other people that sons naturally love, along with mothers, even when the fathers will not step aside or die. Love is essential to the son's role.

Dr. Adler's son is the role Wilhelm has chosen to play in life, the role he has been unable to avoid, the role he has tumbled into even when he tried to escape it. His past record, marred with mistakes, is a story of his efforts to make himself worthy of being Dr. Adler's son without at the same time "outdoing" or even directly competing with his father (28). He tells his father as much: "If anything, I tried too hard. I admit I made many mistakes. Like I thought I shouldn't do things you had done already. Study chemistry. You had done it already. It was in the family" (50). Avoiding thus the distasteful Oedipal competition and yet trying indirectly to match his father's practical success, Tommy, in the early 1930s, turned his back on college after a few semesters to begin a checkered career as actor, hospital orderly, ditchdigger, public relations man, soldier, and toy salesman, a Protean period that, a decade after the war, has left him out of work altogether. No longer a young man, he feels he has failed to match the example of practical success his father set for him. This failure, more than Oedipal guilt, is the source of the anxiety that progressively incapacitates Tommy; he lives in terms of his father's image of him.[4]

As three generations of Depression and post-Depression Americans have discovered, it is increasingly unrealistic and unhealthy to attempt to model oneself after the nineteenth-century American ideal of success Dr. Adler embodies. Pampered, vain, and self-centered, the bland old man thinks of himself as totally self-reliant, a self-made man, the American, Puritan-Protestant business ethic incarnate (50). He fits the familiar Jungian type of the extrovert whom strangers consider a man of civic virtue but whose own children know to be a cruel tyrant.[5] Since Tommy cannot match his father's ideal, Adler rejects him as jittery, dirty, sentimental, weak, immoral, irresponsible: a "slob," the "wrong kind of Jew." Adler calls him the last name even though the doctor, in assimilating himself to the American formula, has given up his own religion (68).

In following in his father's shadow, Tommy has had to make even greater sacrifices, for the practical, extroverted mask of success has forced him to neglect his true, introverted self. In the midst of a very important fit of self-castigation, he gains a glimpse of his other self:

4. Daniel Weiss's position, stated in "Caliban on Prospero: A Psychoanalytic Study on the Novel *Seize the Day,* by Saul Bellow," in *Saul Bellow and the Critics,* ed. Irving Malin (New York, 1967), 114–41, follows the classic Freudian line and argues that Tommy's suffering is the way his superego penalizes him with guilt for having willed his father's death. For a post-Freudian view of the Oedipal wish closer to that of the present position, see Bruno Bettelheim, "The Problem of Generations," in *The Challenge of Youth,* ed. Erik H. Erikson (Garden City, N.Y.), 1965.

5. C. G. Jung, *Psychological Types; or, The Psychology of Individuation,* trans. H. Godwin Baynes (New York, 1933), 435–36, 438–41.

"From his mother he had gotten sensitive feelings, a soft heart, a brooding nature, a tendency to be confused under pressure" (25). It is this self that feels rather than judges, this "feminine" quality, that Tommy has been unable to accept, even though it is the dominant side of his personality, because he has not been able to cast off "his father's opinion of him." This he tried to do as an actor in California when he "cast off his father's name" and became Tommy Wilhelm rather than Wilhelm Adler. But the name change belonged to his earliest effort to match his father's success without directly imitating it and thus was, ironically, determined by his father's opinion of him. As a consequence, he never succeeded "in feeling like Tommy" and remained always, in his soul, Wilky. Wilky, he fears, is "his inescapable self," a doleful state of things for which he has developed an elaborate biological explanation; he thinks: "There's really very little that a man can change at will. . . . He can't overthrow the government or be differently born" (24–25). This explanation may seem to be a rationalization that does not fit Tommy's case, but it indicates nonetheless that he feels he has reached the limit of his capacity to change his external self in order to gratify his father.

The real source of his anxiety is the double bind Dr. Adler has forced him into—a bind that keeps him alienated from any of his inward selves: Tommy, Wilhelm, Wilky, and others still unconscious. If, on the one hand, he attempts to follow his father's example of practical self-reliance, he commits the crime of freedom against his father and remains tormented by his father's godlike voice internalized as conscience: "The changed name [Tommy] was a mistake, and he would admit it as freely as you liked. But this mistake couldn't be undone now, so why must his father continually remind him how he had sinned?" (25). If, on the other hand, he feels as though he might really be Wilky, which has been his father's name for him for forty years, he sees himself through Adler's view of Wilky-like softness and introversion: "When he was drunk he reproached himself horribly as Wilky. 'You fool, you clunk, you Wilky!' he called himself" (25). It is not unhealthy to be a Wilky, but it is sick to judge one's own self so harshly. Thus separated from the vital center of his personality, his inner *daimon,* Tommy seems doomed to follow a path of progressively destructive self-judgment until at last all his creative possibilities are dead.

This is not the psychic reality Bellow has described, however, for he concurs with Jung that the personality runs contrary ways. Especially at middle age, where Tommy now stands, does the personality, like everything, "run into its opposite." Today is the day of reckoning when Tommy must undergo what Jung calls "enantiodromia," the psychological process of "being torn asunder into pairs of opposites" (*TE*, 82–83). Dr. Tamkin, in most things the opposite of Dr. Adler, represents to Tommy the Spirit of Alternatives holding out to him an alternative self. To reach this new self, however, the old must die.

Dr. Tamkin speaks for the unconscious attitude that Tommy as an introvert and a loser cannot see in himself but projects on external objects. According to Jung, the unconscious contents of the psyche stand in a compensatory relationship to those that are conscious. Because an introvert fails to give external objects the importance they possess, "a compensatory relation to the object develops in the unconscious, which makes itself felt in consciousness as an unconditional and irrepressible tie to the object." Since the unconscious drives of an introvert are thus extroverted, the object develops "an overwhelming influence . . . because it seizes upon the individual unawares." Such powerlessness before external forces is typical for Wilhelm: "After much thought and hesitation and debate he invariably took the course he had rejected innumerable times. Ten such decisions made up the history of his life" (23). Because the introvert attaches little conscious value to his external actions, his unconscious needs often get him "swamped in inferior relationships, and his desire to dominate [the external world with his mind or emotions] ends in a pitiful craving to be loved."[6] Thus Tommy, who has good reasons to suspect Tamkin of being a sham and a confidence man, finds himself nonetheless unable to resist the man's financial schemes. "He had resolved not to invest money with Tamkin, and then had given him a check" (23).

Bellow's image of Dr. Tamkin has been called "one of the most singular condemnations in contemporary literature of what modern man has become." But even those who have judged Tamkin most severely, or who have been puzzled by his role, have not missed the irony that the most profound insights come from his mouth and that he is "wise, accurate psychologically, and responsible for Wilhelm's final enlightenment."[7] We would be wise not to judge Tamkin too harshly, since

6. *Ibid.*, 477–78; *TE*, 186; Jung, *Psychological Types*, 478.

7. William J. Handy, "Saul Bellow and the Naturalistic Hero," *Texas Studies in Literature and Language*, V (Winter, 1964), 542; Weiss, "Caliban on Prospero," 138.

we see him only through a tissue of qualities Tommy has projected on him. If Tamkin did not exist, Tommy would have had to invent him so that there would be someone upon whom he might project the unacknowledged contents of his own psyche.

The qualities projected by the introvert's unconscious "are primarily infantile and archaic" ones, the primitive contents that find expression in the Jungian archetypes. Consequently, the objects that receive such projections seem endowed with terrifying "magical powers." The archetype Tommy projects onto Tamkin is the important figure of the magician, a dominant of the collective unconscious embodying ego-inflating psychic energies that are capable of producing what Jung calls "the mana-personality" (*TE,* 240–41). Tommy sees Tamkin variously as a "benevolent magician" (81), as "shrewd, and wizardlike, patronizing, secret, potent" (64), and as a "faker" (punning perhaps with fakir) who "knows what he's talking about" (98). As products of a projected psychic energy that is morally neutral, spirit-figures are notorious for their moral ambivalence. Jung says of them that "we can never know what evil may not be necessary in order to produce good by enantiodromia, and what good may very possibly lead to evil." In dreams the spirit-figure may appear simultaneously as a "white magician" dressed in a long black robe and as a "black magician" clothed in a white robe, an archetypal equivalent of the paradox that Tamkin cons Tommy out of his last seven hundred dollars while guiding him toward the birth of his real self. Ethical neutrality enables the magician-figure to break through the sort of bind that incapacitates Tommy. "The archetype of spirit in the shape of a man always appears in a situation where insight, understanding, good advice, determination, planning, etc., are needed but cannot be mustered on one's own resources," Jung writes. "The archetype compensates this state of spiritual deficiency by contents designed to fill the gap."[8]

Tommy's need for a new life, more than Tamkin's greed, lies at the bottom of the irresistible attraction this self-taught healer of humanity holds for Dr. Adler's son (95). For Adler's rational dogmatism, Tamkin substitutes an appealingly intuitive view of things: a "keen nose for things in the bud pregnant with future promise," an "eye . . .

8. Jung, *Psychological Types,* 479–80; C. G. Jung, *The Archetypes and the Collective Unconscious,* trans. R. F. C. Hull (New York, 1959), 215–16.

constantly ranging for new possibilities," to use Jung's description of the type.[9] Tamkin's brand of extroversion stands as a bridge between Adler's absolutism and Tommy's introversion. Tamkin's long-range goal (aside from fleecing Tommy) seems to be to help him convert his self-image from slob to "king" (75–77). To reach this goal he must first alter Wilhelm's set of mind.

To prepare Tommy, Tamkin supplies him with readings, advice, informal lectures, and mental exercises. A sympathetic surrogate father (though no more than ten years older than his victim/son) who understands the heart, he teaches Tommy to value his emotions, rather than despise them, as a way to overcome loneliness, suffering, and the death-wish (97–99). When, "under Dr. Tamkin's influence," Wilhelm begins "to remember the poems he used to read," they come back to him in pairs dealing with death (William Shakespeare's "That time of year thou mayst in me behold") and rebirth ("Lycidas"), foreshadowing the pattern of his own development (12–13). In order to counter Wilhelm's obsessive anxieties about the past (his father and mother) and about the future (the market and his sons), Tamkin proposes "here-and-now" mental exercises to immerse him totally in the present (61, 89–90). By focusing his attention on increasingly small concrete details and thus driving anxiety from his consciousness, Tommy is supposed to achieve a state of pure being in which the "present, present, eternal present, like a big, huge, giant wave—colossal, bright and beautiful, full of life and death, climbing into the sky, standing in the seas," will break upon him (89).

Tamkin's immersion theory of self-discovery provides at base a method for releasing dammed-up emotions, as all the water imagery in the book implies.[10] In the language of Jung, Tamkin will use Tommy's secondary faculty for introverted sensation to develop his suppressed capacity for feeling. In this intermediate stage of sensation, with his mind fastened intensely on an irresistible object, Tommy will, according to Jung, see the same thing as anyone else, but his mind will not stop "at the purely objective effect"; it will concern itself instead "with the subjective perception released by the objective stimulus."

9. Jung, *Psychological Types,* 464.

10. Clinton W. Trowbridge, in "Water Imagery in *Seize the Day,*" *Critique: Studies in Modern Fiction,* IX (1966–67), 62–73, argues this very convincingly.

This subjective content will include mythological images, primal possibilities, and dispositions of the collective unconscious, all hints of an archaic reality within.[11]

Bellow the trained anthropologist has turned up a rich store of myth-laden particulars (mythemes) that Bellow the novelist uses to give the sense that Wilhelm might at any moment turn a corner and break through into the mirror world of the collective unconscious. Aside from the sense that the entire novel has been set underwater so that the Hotel Gloriana resembles a submerged Mount Olympus, Dr. Adler, a submarine Zeus or Jehovah, and Tommy's day, a descent into the waters of rebirth, there is a constant bombardment of mythemes that intensifies as Tamkin carries Tommy toward the climax of his enantiodromia.[12] For Tommy, the commodity market is literally a great mechanical wheel of fortune that rises and falls with the seasons (78). The various father-figures (Adler, Rappaport, Tamkin) become gods who need only speak a word to provide the key that will liberate Tommy from his misery (87, 109). He begins to think of himself in terms of mythic animals: as bear, the symbol of prime matter and instincts (23); as bull, the figure of fertility and chthonic power (76); as hippopotamus, the river horse, to the Egyptians a figure for strength, vigor, fertility and water (6); and, in his son's language, as "hummuspotamus," a river of humus, source of organic life (29). Street markets become cornucopias, and a gilded cafeteria metamorphoses into a dreamscape: "Whole fishes were framed like pictures with carrots, and the salads were like terraced landscapes or like Mexican pyramids; slices of lemon and onion and radishes were like sun and moon and stars; . . . the cakes [were] swollen as if sleepers had baked them in their dreams" (91). A panicked trip to Tamkin's room followed by an elevator ride to the basement massage room takes on the proportions of an ascent to the zenith and a descent to the underworld (106–108).

As Tamkin's teachings about the need to kill the "pretender soul" in order to liberate one's "real soul" (terms very close to the Jungian "persona" or "ego" and "the Self") sink in, Wilhelm begins to catch glimpses of the collective nature of this real soul; his "involuntary feelings" about the "larger body" of humanity break through to con-

11. Jung, *Psychological Types*, 516, 499–503.

12. Trowbridge, "Water Imagery," 62–73.

sciousness.[13] A dark tunnel beneath Times Square becomes the collective unconscious externalized: "In the . . . tunnel . . . all of a sudden, unsought, a general love for all these imperfect and lurid-looking people burst out in Wilhelm's breast. . . . They were his brothers and his sisters. He was imperfect and disfigured himself, but what difference did that make if he was united with them by this blaze of love?" (84–85). For Jung, it is the "sense of solidarity with the world" accompanying the assimilation of the collective elements of the unconscious that enables many sick individuals for the first time to love and be loved and thus marks the turning point of their treatment (*TE,* 158).

Within this larger body, Tommy, who regrets that in a city like New York "the fathers [are] no fathers and the sons no sons" (84), discovers the role his real soul seems to be meant to play, a complex one combining important attributes of the archetypal son. Early in the novel he thinks of himself as a sacrificial son, a secular Isaac/Christ whose suffering gives life to others: "When I had it, I flowed money. They bled it away from me. I hemorrhaged money" (40, 76). By itself this role is totally unsatisfying; it belongs to his view of himself as loser and victim, an image he owes to his father. If the son must be sacrificed, he should, at least, be beloved and lamented.

Under Tamkin's instruction he comes to the threshold of a second attribute of the son archetype, the previously unacknowledged Oedipal hatred. With Wilhelm's mother dead, the rivalry between father and son has shifted to the other treasure that fathers, especially in a gerontocracy like the Gloriana, hoard from their sons, money. Midway through the novel, in an argument with Adler, Wilhelm bursts out: "By God, you have to admit it. The money makes the difference." He then continues: "Just keep your money. . . . Keep it and enjoy it yourself. That's the ticket!" (55). This rivalry produces another of those feelings he experiences that emerge involuntarily from the collective unconscious. He is discussing the possibility of his father's death with Tamkin. When Tamkin asks whether he loves his father, he answers, "Of course." Then Bellow adds: "As he said this there was a great pull at the very center of his soul. When a fish strikes the line you feel the

13. *TE,* 250; M.-L. von Franz, "The Process of Individuation," in *Man and His Symbols,* ed. Carl G. Jung (Garden City, N.Y., 1970), 161–62.

live force in your hand. A mysterious being beneath the water, driven by hunger, has taken the hook and rushes away and fights, writhing" (92–93). The fish struggling under the waters of consciousness must be a negative or mixed answer to Tamkin's question, a shadowy awareness for the first time that his love for Adler is not innocent of hate and that his desire to see his father live is not free of the contrary wish. This is the great feeling Wilhelm must confront and cannot, until Tamkin teaches him to seize the day.

As guru, Tamkin can neither tell nor show Wilhelm what he needs to know but can only lead him to the threshold and hope he will take the final step, make the necessary connections. It is in panicked pursuit of Tamkin that Wilhelm, cut off from all other worldly connections, stumbles at the end into the huge funeral line that carries him toward the consummation of his heart's ultimate need (115). He is trying to get his money back. Instead he undergoes the most unrestrained, powerful, and intensely personal emotional experience of his life, one that stirs him to the vital center of his personality. At the same time as Tamkin's running away breaks Wilhelm's dependence on him as a surrogate father, it leads the client and victim toward the most irresistible object his mind will ever fasten on and thus brings his immersion in the here-and-now to the highest intensity possible.

When Wilhelm's place in the funeral line reaches the coffin, there is a catch in his breath, and he finds himself "so struck" that he cannot "go away" (116–17). As he stands by the dead man and his eyes begin to shine with tears, the most essential contents of his unconscious, images and associations released by this objective stimulus, flow forth. At first he sees the dead stranger as gray-haired, proper but not old, calling to Wilhelm's mind his father and the Oedipal wish to see him dead. Then the corpse becomes "a man—another human creature," an association that focuses the general sense of solidarity with mankind he had earlier felt in the dark tunnel beneath Times Square. Into this collective image the more particular one breaks again as he addresses the stranger as "Father" and calls on him (or is it his mistress Olive?) to protect him "against that devil who wants [his] life." Initially "that devil" seems to be his parasitic wife Margaret, but as he continues to speak to the corpse, the devil becomes his father: "If you want it [my life], then kill me. Take, take it, take it from me." This thought carries him to the furthest depth of the hatred that divides him from his father.[14] It also causes him to see himself (probably the Wilky-self his father created) as the dead man and carries him "past words, past reason, coherence" to "the source of all tears": the pure intimate self-pity that comes with the thought of one's own death.

Somewhere well past reason, in the archaic content he has projected on the dead stranger, Tommy has become the center of a wild cult of lamentation. As the chief mourner at a huge funeral for his father, himself, and all mankind, he sees "the flowers and lights fused ecstatically" in his wet eyes and hears "heavy sea-like music." Then, like Tammuz or Osiris, ancient son-gods and sacrificial quickeners of new life, he feels the sea of lamentation pour into him as he sinks "deeper than sorrow," where he must await rebirth. In his descent into the archetypal unconscious, Tommy seems to approach most closely Tammuz or Dumuzi, the oldest known vegetation god in the Western tradition. As the power in sap of trees and plants, this god died at the end of spring and was lamented throughout ancient Mesopotamia by wailing women who regarded him variously as a dying son, brother, and husband. From Tammuz Bellow may have derived the names Tommy, Tam-kin, and even Wilhelm's self-reproachful "dummy," as well as the water and descent imagery, the temporal setting (early summer), and the struggle between age and youth, death and rebirth.[15]

Identified thus with the archetypal contents of the collective unconscious, a "chaos of instinct and spirit," he becomes united with his real self, the god or king hidden within him. How well he will, in the future, assimilate this "sunken power" and work out roles that acknowledge both his own psychic needs and the limits on self-expression created by society depends on the extent to which he understands a lesson Tamkin gave him earlier on the value of symbolic actions. In that episode Tommy is complaining about the way his wife Margaret lives only "in order to punish him." Tamkin interjects the story of his own wife: she was a "painful alcoholic" whom he loved deeply and "tried everything in [his] power to cure." But, he continues, he failed and she drowned, apparently a suicide. Wilhelm, whose distrust is especially

14. *Cf.* Bellow, *Seize the Day,* 54, where Adler gives his son the impression that he resents the thought his son will still be alive after Adler, "the better man of the two," is dead.

15. See James G. Frazer, *The Golden Bough* (New York, 1951), 378–80, and Thorkild Jacobsen, "Toward the Image of Tammuz," *History of Religion,* I (Winter, 1961), 189–213.

intense at this moment, attacks Tamkin in his mind: "Liar! . . . He invented a woman and killed her off and then called himself a healer" (94–95).

Wilhelm is probably right that this is one of Tamkin's lies or phantasies, but being a liar does not keep Tamkin from being a healer. The ability to produce, recognize, and "kill off" phantasies or symbols of man's deepest anxieties—guilt about failure, Oedipal hatreds, need for security, wish to be loved, fear of his own death—furnishes the key to the method that witch doctors, priests, psychoanalysts, and sane individuals all employ. "The only person who escapes the grim law of enantiodromia is the man who knows how to separate himself from the unconscious, not by repressing it . . . but by putting it clearly before him [often in symbolic form] as *that which he is not*" because its fears and needs are the burden of all mankind (*TE,* 83).

What lies immediately ahead for Tommy then is the sort of differentiation pursued in this essay, a process in which he may discover that the sources of the phantasies he experienced by the stranger's coffin lie in the collective mind of man and through this realization free himself of their destructive personal influence. It is well Bellow stopped with Tommy's phantasies, for lies that tell the deepest human truths are the most powerful tools a novelist can ever hope to control. They are Tommy's inner resources. Phantasies that arise from the core, as his do, provide raw material for transformations that go much deeper than roles taken out of the air, from the external world, the way Wilhelm Adler became Tommy Wilhelm, actor, orderly, ditchdigger, public relations man, soldier, and salesman. Such, at least, is the limit Bellow's next novel, *Henderson the Rain King,* places on lasting personal change.

MODELS, MIRRORS, AND TOTEMIC ALCHEMY

Although its characters and settings differ, *Henderson the Rain King,* published in 1959, is very much a thematic, structural, and psychological sequel to *Seize the Day.* Eugene H. Henderson begins in much the same condition that Tommy Wilhelm ended, overwhelmed by his emotions, at the end of his rope, eager to begin a new life if only he can find one. At the funeral of the dead stranger, Tommy, stripped of his last assets, receives the final blow that will launch his progress out of his wretched present life if he can begin to understand all the deep meanings projected on the corpse and, by understanding, reclaim the inner powers formerly projected on his wife, his father, and Dr. Tamkin. In the opening chapters of Henderson's story, the hero receives a number of blows, literal and figurative, that send him forth on what such critics as Victor Pribanic and Mark Winchell have recognized as Joseph Campbell's monomyth of the heroic quest built around a departure, an initiation, and a return.[16] Whether we read the novel from the Jungian perspective that supports Campbell's monomyth or from the Reichian point of view as other critics have (Eusebio Rodrigues, M. Gilbert Porter, and Helge Nilson, for example), the psychological meaning of Henderson's quest is clear. Like Wilhelm's, Henderson's present life is a mess. His persona (Jung) or character armor (Reich) is inadequate. The shock of his trip to Africa opens him to new archetypal roles (Jung) and to the primal energy heretofore locked away deep within him (Reich). He returns from Africa a new man, more or less.

The degree of Henderson's change is the moot point, one demanding close attention to the text. Whereas some critics speak of his "complete therapeutic transformation" or his full regeneration, others are more cautious. Nilson, for example, argues that Bellow's attitude toward Reichian solutions to Henderson's problems is "ironic and comic." Astrid Holm, who sees Henderson's quest from the perspective of Sartre's existentialism, concludes that the hero's transformation is incomplete, that he "has not changed very much" and is "still essentially egotistic" and thus that the novel is open ended. Rather than choose between Sartre and Reich, or even the American Transcendentalists, as the major influence on the novel, I prefer to concede the likely impact of all three and thereby acknowledge the complexity of Bellow's book.[17] At the same time, I would like to examine the specific nature of Bellow's original blend of phenomenology (from Sartre) and psychology (via Reich) by looking in detail at Henderson's interac-

16. Saul Bellow, *Henderson the Rain King,* in *The Portable Saul Bellow* (New York, 1974), 160; hereinafter cited parenthetically by page number in the text.

17. Rodrigues, "Reichianism in *Henderson the Rain King,*" 213; M. Gilbert Porter, *Whence the Power? The Artistry and Humanity of Saul Bellow* (Columbia, Mo., 1974), 144; Nilson, "Saul Bellow and Wilhelm Reich," 81; Astrid Holm, "Existentialism and Saul Bellow's *Henderson, the Rain King,*" *American Studies in Scandinavia,* X (1978), 106–108.

tions with Dahfu, the Wariri king who becomes his initiator, mentor, deceiver, and psychotherapist.

The essence of Dahfu's message is the need and possibility of personality change (382). Dahfu's position seems an odd emphasis coming from a writer whose previous novel argued eloquently for the limits biology places on the individual's capacity for change. In *Seize the Day,* as we saw, Tommy Wilhelm decides his attempts to alter his personality by changing his name were mistakes: "A man . . . can't change his lungs, or nerves, or constitution or temperament. They're not under his control. When he's young and strong and impulsive and dissatisfied with the way things are he wants to rearrange them to assert his freedom. He can't overthrow the government or be differently born" (24). Although Tommy's final breakdown may, as John Clayton says, amount in Reichian terms to "a healing surrender of the armored self," the extent of his eventual change remains problematical.[18]

Henderson, in contrast, believes that he is a Becomer (321), the opposite of Be-ers like Willatale, the queen of the Arnewi (291), and Dahfu himself (321). *Becoming* he associates less with Sartrean freedom than with the anguish Sartre assigns to the unending change, the "necessity of continually choosing" oneself, that Sartre takes for freedom.[19] For Henderson feels driven to his constant becoming by the "disturbance in [his] heart, a voice that [speaks] there and [says], 'I want, I want, I want!' "(161). Dahfu sets out, however, to invert Henderson's view of change. Dahfu believes that it is "never too late for any man to change, no matter how fully formed," that even a confused individual in his middle fifties like Henderson can "absorb lion qualities" (382). To Dahfu, the capacity for becoming is not a disturbance in the heart but a cause for hope.

Dahfu's hope of absorbing lion qualities clues the reader to the sort of change the novel explores. The king intends to use models from which Henderson will absorb new powers. It is with Dahfu's theory of modeling that the questions about the degree of Henderson's change arise, for the action of the book only partly supports his optimistic theory. The novel shows Bellow drawing an essential distinction between the roles played in personality growth by models on the one hand and mirrors on the other. By helping us understand the limit

18. John Clayton, *Saul Bellow: In Defense of Man* (Bloomington, 1968), 133.

19. Sartre, *Being and Nothingness,* 628.

Bellow places on the king's theory, this distinction between modeling and mirroring determines the degree to which Dahfu is finally a dramatic character rather than Bellow's Reichian spokesman—a character we can get behind rather than simply accept uncritically.

To contemporary critics Dahfu may appear to be grounded in Sartre and Reich, but his intellectual tradition runs back through Trofim Lysenko (Joseph Stalin's "dictator" of biology and agronomy), Jean-Baptiste Lamarck, and Jean-Jacques Rousseau, to John Locke. Dahfu's notions about change show him to be a thoroughgoing environmentalist (and therefore the diametrical opposite of Tommy Wilhelm when Tommy stresses biological fixity). Dahfu's tradition is clear to Henderson, for he ties the king to Lamarck and to his own collegiate memories of having laughed at the French naturalist's "bourgeois ideas" (415). This connection to Lamarck arises from the Frenchman's theory that individuals and species change through acquired characteristics, that is, through environmental influences, including models like those Dahfu proposes. As a rich boy, Henderson apparently laughed at Lamarck because Henderson assumed that heredity, surely economic and seemingly biological inheritance, determined his own behavior.

It is odd, however, that Henderson accepted his teacher's view that Lamarck's theories were bourgeois; for in the twentieth century, when Western biology subscribed to genetic theories of change, the chief defenders of Lamarckian theory were Soviet scientists, led (for the most part, disastrously) by Lysenko. The political and psychological reasons for Lysenko's or Dahfu's embracing the influence of acquired characteristics are fairly obvious. It is much easier to change the environment than the genetic material. Environmental theories are also more democratic. Altering genetic determinants is exceedingly slow, hence conservative. Optimists and revolutionaries, of necessity, want to believe environmental theories of change. If acquired characteristics could be inherited, as Lamarck and Darwin thought, individuals, economies, cultures could progress almost before one's eyes. No wonder Henderson, who at midlife tells himself, "I must change," and "I must not live on the past, it will ruin me" (415), longs earnestly to accept Dahfu's theory of positive models.

Dahfu's position, as Henderson's career demonstrates, has its good points, for models seem to play a distinct role in determining Henderson's range of behaviors. Building on his foreign studies, the king cites

William James and others when he speaks of "the transformation of human material" in language that suggests Bellow may have Ralph Ellison's Protean character Rinehart in mind. Dahfu contends that transformation can "work either way, either from the rind to the core or from the core to the rind" (364). His emphasis here would suggest, if we identified the rind with the external world and the core with genes, that he assigns heredity a role equal to environment. But as Henderson summarizes Dahfu's position, it is otherwise; he speaks instead of "the flesh influencing the mind, the mind influencing the flesh, back again to the mind, back once more to the flesh" (364). Here, as Dahfu's examples and subsequent explanations show, both flesh and mind are, in an important sense, external. He believes that the flesh adapts itself to influences surrounding it (365), while the conceptions the mind holds, which can include images taken from the external world, influence the flesh (396). Little wonder, then, that Henderson, so eagerly desiring change, finds his conversations with Dahfu ablaze with loftiness (344).

Building on hunches as well as on his education, Dahfu intuits a system of noble Proteanism in which man, "the prince of organisms," the "master of adaptations," an "artist of suggestions," becomes his own "principal work of art," a triumphant miracle (365). Drawing on an ontology that since Descartes, if not since Plato, has blurred the distinction between knowledge and being, Dahfu asserts that not only psychosomatic diseases originate in the brain but "*everything* originated there" (365). As Dahfu says, in language that parallels Lacan's view of hysteria, "Disease is a speech of the psyche" (366), but, he stresses, disease is not the only language the psyche uses. It can also speak of hope and the spirit, for the body expresses whatever "orders and directives" the cerebral cortex sends out (366). Consequently, if one wishes to express a "noble self-conception" in the flesh, it is essential to have "a desirable model in the cortex" (396). In achieving this noble end, human imagination becomes an essential "force of nature" (399). For Dahfu, what mankind imagines it becomes: "The career of our specie . . . is evidence that one imagination after another grows literal. . . . All human accomplishment has this same origin, identically. . . . What Homo sapiens imagines, he may slowly convert himself to" (399).

Because models in the cortex thus govern behavior, the lion has an important part to play for Henderson. The lion is the counterforce to fear, and fear, Dahfu claims, has great power: "[It] is a ruler of mankind. It has the biggest dominion of all. . . . As a molding force it comes second only to Nature itself" (386). Whatever the universal validity of Dahfu's claim, it accurately describes Henderson. But for Henderson, who is occasionally too dauntless in dealing with the external world, fear seems to be chiefly metaphysical and psychological. Although he feels he is "just about kissing cousins" with death, "ultra-familiar" (305), his fear of it is nonetheless normal for a man in his middle fifties (157, 313, 380–81).[20] In addition to death, Henderson appears to fear himself: he is a big man with large brawling emotions (143) and a considerable amount of hostile energy that he has to work to keep under control, as his talk of sublimating blows into truth indicates (160–61).

Although Henderson does not make the connection, his fears are likely tied to the view of himself he received from his father. He implies at the start that much of his low self-esteem comes from his not being worthy of the "three million dollars after taxes" he inherited (141). When he thinks thus of himself as a bum, he turns for help to the books left him by his father (141–42). That he usually finds the currency his father used as bookmarks suggests that money is the chief legacy he will ever receive from his father. Money is not what he needs; it simply breeds more guilt.

That in one of his father's books he also finds a passage, seemingly marked by currency, that reads, "The forgiveness of sins is perpetual and righteousness first is not required" (141–42) implies something quite different about what he has inherited. To have marked this passage, his father, too, must have been seeking a way out of his own sense of unworthiness. His father's need for forgiveness is probably the cause, possibly an effect, of the elder Henderson's scholarly interest in the Albigenses, on whom he wrote a famous book (145). As members of a Catharistic sect of southern France between the eleventh and thirteenth centuries, the Albigenses aspired to a transcendent purity that rejected the material creation as evil. His interest in them suggests that Henderson's father, like his friends William James and Henry Adams (145), struggled with the demands of a rigid puritan conscience.

That the father could be overly judgmental, even morally cruel, be-

20. Holm, "Existentialism and Bellow's *Henderson the Rain King*," 96–97.

comes clear when Henderson recalls, late in the novel after his self-image is strong enough to tolerate the thought, that on the day of the funeral of his older brother Dick his father swore at him, "put aside his customary elegance of words" to curse his surviving son (463). Henderson rationalizes this lapse from eloquence as a result of his failing to comfort his father in his grief (463). But he then internalizes the curse; it is further evidence that his father might have preferred that Henderson had died and Dick lived so that the father was not left "alone in the world" with the less worthy son (171).

Damaging messages from his father, more than his large frame and brawling emotions, have left Henderson with a weakened sense of himself, an ego poorly prepared to deal with the usual demands of life. The image of himself he inherited is too weak to tolerate the fears that normal men and women face daily. His instincts, therefore, are accurate when they send him to the violin in pursuit of his "father's spirit" (167), in search of a new, more supportive message. As with his father, however, the violin can only express his grief and his protest against his wretched condition. To renew his sense of himself he needs, in addition, a good enough father to help him internalize a healthy self-image. Because his need is what it is, it leads him eventually to Atti, Dahfu, and the spirit of Dahfu's father, which Dahfu seeks in the male lion, Gmilo (359).

Given Henderson's problems, the lion Atti is an especially apt model for him to take. For Atti triggers his fear (352), terrifies him with his mortality (355), stimulates the guilt of his hostility to cats (354; *cf.* 225–26), and, through her physical presence, allows Henderson to experience his fear to its fullest and thereby learn to live with it (389). Atti is at the same time a perfect model of "utmost power," combining a potential for destruction with animal grace and immense control (356). She is a splendid shot of the animal nature that mankind, especially Henderson, needs (380). He must therefore "imitate or dramatize the behavior of lions" (391) in his own flesh in order for such nobility to work its way to his mind and then back to the flesh as a new, nobler personality (394). Following Dahfu's instructions and example, he outwardly becomes the lion: he gives it everything he has and roars his head off (395–96). He accepts Dahfu's notion that change "must be possible" (404) yet figures he will "never make a lion" (425).

Henderson, it turns out, is right to have reservations about the ultimate success of Dahfu's theory. As Dahfu's death and his plan to trick Henderson into succeeding him indicate (438–39, 442–43), the king himself is not all he pretends to be. His teachings apparently contain an element of deception or, Henderson decides, of self-deception (425).

Despite the deceptions, though, Dahfu's theory is not totally wrong. He has simply confused modeling with mirroring. That something other than modeling is taking place in Henderson's work with Dahfu becomes clear when we notice the ways Henderson responds to the king and Atti. When their conversations are loftiest, Henderson's reactions go well beyond the stimuli Dahfu supplies: "I saw things not double or triple merely, but in countless outlines of wavering color, gold, red, green, umber. . . . Sometimes Dahfu seemed to be three times his size, with the spectrum around him. Larger than life, he loomed over me and spoke with more than one voice" (344–45). Or again, Henderson notices "the extra shadow of brilliance . . . the sign of an intenser gift of being" the king carries with him (353). When Henderson finally touches Atti, he thinks his "nails [become] like five burning tapers" and the "bones of the hand [become] incandescent" (356).

These moments of heightened emotion are not energies in Dahfu and Atti that Henderson becomes or takes into himself as one would according to Dahfu's modeling (or Sartre's phenomenological) theory of becoming. These are energies already in Henderson but locked away beneath his distrust and fear of himself. Much of his life he has searched for a father or a hero to give him direction (142). Because he lacks a focus, his emotional life remains blocked within; he is full of the static energy he ascribes to Atti. Dahfu and Atti do not give new powers to Henderson. They simply mirror, in an elemental psychological sense, what is already there: Henderson's potential, hungry for expression, driving him through the disorder of his life. Dahfu's theory optimistically places too much emphasis on environmental causes of change and not enough on the inner material with which outward forces must work.

Ultimately Henderson's capacity for change runs up against the limit of inner material. At the moment when Dahfu tells him he should feel his lionhood, what Henderson instead feels is his earlier tie to pigs: "Lions for him, pigs for me. I wish I was dead" (396). He remembers two sows that used to follow him (397), even before he, rather perversely and anti-Semitically, chose to start a pig farm (157–58). "Those animals have become a part of me," he told his first wife (398). It is with his inner pighood that Henderson has to work, for his early animal friends mirrored something large, self-indulgent, low, clumsy, and childish in him.

Because the totem animals of the Arnewi tribe, cattle (192), bear some relationship to the pig, Henderson was able to feel a basic kinship with that group of large, usually peaceful folk. But cattle are closer to sheep in temperament (*árnos* is Greek for sheep) than to incessantly rooting pigs, and it was Henderson's nosing into their way of life as the grandiose, Western-activist saviour and his blowing up their cistern (242–43) that separated him from that excessively Rousseauistic tribe. The Hobbesian Wariri (war-weary) with their lions effectively mirror the truculence lurking beneath Henderson's imperfectly controlled exterior. In contrast to the generous, meek, good Arnewi (297), the Wariri are smaller, darker, tougher, more violent and sadistic (250, 288, 331, 343). Much as the Wariri keep a wild beast beneath their palace (281), Henderson keeps violence locked away in his heart. When he tries to deny it, it erupts clumsily, as in the explosion of the Arnewi's cistern. When he acknowledges his own darker side, however, and allows his "barbaric emotions" a place in consciousness, they express themselves as the strength, courage, and spiritual force he demonstrates for the Wariri when he utters "a roar like the great Assyrian bull" (302). This spontaneous gesture indicates that the transmutation of his personality has progressed from the pigs of his past and the cattle of the Arnewi well along the way to the force and beauty of Atti.

The reader who wishes to understand the totemic alchemy taking place within Henderson's psyche must be willing to do what Henderson does, literally and in the order of Henderson's development: imitate the sounds of the animals he has allowed to mirror his inner world. The reader who has the comic courage to oink and grunt like a pig, to moo like a cow, to bellow like a bull, and then roar like Atti will likely experience the direction of Henderson's transformation. Such change begins in the rind, the flesh, but it affects the core, the psyche. As the dross of the oink and moo drop from one's spirit, the fire of finer feeling liberates the gold of the lion within. Like Henderson's, the reader's spirit may be altered.

This comic alchemy, however, is finally a matter of mirrors rather than models. Henderson's transformations remain temporary, mere imitations of models, unless the utterances sound a dominant chord within his being. If the sound strikes what is deep inside, a true and permanent change occurs. Distinguishing Dahfu's models from effective psychological mirroring enables us therefore to measure the likelihood that Henderson's transformation may last.

Even at the height of his identification with Dahfu (423) and Atti, Henderson remains convinced that he is deceiving himself, that he will "never make a lion" (425). He thinks that he may, however, make "a small gain here and there in the attempt" (425). This progress is what Dahfu, in fact, has asked of him, that he "try to make more of a lion" of himself (401). Consequently, following Dahfu's death (439), when Henderson escapes with his life from the Wariri, he carries the lion cub—a little of the lion, a little of Dahfu (453)—with him. That much of the Wariri totem he has absorbed. On the plane, though, he gives the cub he has named Dahfu to the lonely boy from Persia, whom Henderson describes as "a black-haired boy, like my own" (461). Literally he means the boy has hair like his own son's, but there are parallel associations to Henderson's own "hair like Persian lambs' fur" (142) and therefore to the sheep qualities of the Arnewi. In effect, then, on the plane he combines reminders of the two parts of his African adventure, the warrior Wariri and the gentle Arnewi, mirrors of two dominating energies within his personality.

It is this union of opposites that, in the dream logic of the ending (and of the entire novel), brings him a fourth totem animal. During his return flight, his memory does him "a great favor," grants him "certain recollections" that make a "sizable difference" to him (462). One of these is the memory of his father's curse (463). Immediately after this courageous recollection comes a memory of his stay in Ontario. He remembers working with Smolak, the old brown bear with whom he rode the roller coaster (464). Although Smolak is a "poor broken ruined creature" and an outcast, Henderson takes comfort from recollections of his relationship to the animal: "Before pigs ever came on my horizon, I received a deep impression from a bear. . . . I [was] enbeared by him. . . . I didn't come to the pigs as a tabula rasa. . . . Something deep already was inscribed on me" (464).

Nor did he come to Smolak a tabula rasa. Although events in the novel do not show whether Smolak appealed to qualities in Henderson that had a genetic source on the one hand or a developmental origin on the other, Henderson's past places a firm limit on the total plasticity or Protean nature of his personality. He cannot become whatever he is conscious of, as Sartre's notion of being-for-itself implies; he can only become whatever he is mirrored by. Both bear and pigs speak to an essential dimension of the man.

As a totemic mirror, the bear, Henderson realizes, carries a kinship to pigs: "Pigs don't have a monopoly on grunting" (462). Like Henderson and pigs, bears are large, hungry creatures, often surly, uncouth, shambling. But a bear's roar is nearer the lion's, as are its teeth, fur, and generally noble manner. Through his memory of Smolak, Henderson discovers a truer totem, one more perfectly mirroring his own personality than did the pigs, cats, octopus, cows, bull, and lion that in turn mirrored some part of him. The bear as totem forgives what is clumsy in Henderson while it acknowledges his noble qualities. For these and other essential reasons, it is the bear he loves (464). Whatever Henderson loves he holds in his cortex (the way totem groups do) as the mirror of a power in himself, and so he becomes what he loves. The projections of Henderson's noble narcissism, by finding mirrors of the self in the outer world, succeed where Dahfu's theory of models partially fails.

The final scene, which takes place in Henderson's mind, with Henderson, the boy from Persia, and the cub galloping in frozen Newfoundland around the "riveted body of the plane" (466), would be absurd in the usual novel of realism. But in a dream book like *Henderson the Rain King,* which reports from the other side of the clouds (178–79) about things that "happened as in a dream" (159; *cf.* 298, 301, 319), the boundless energy of Henderson makes perfect sense. The plane is the bound self that belongs to his past. His energy is the gift of integration. Henderson's new power is what he possesses in place of the emotional chaos that swallowed Tommy at the stranger's funeral.

Henderson's energy is the product of bringing together the conscious and unconscious halves of his being, of accurate mirroring and growth. It stands in bold opposition to what we find in later novels such as Pynchon's *V.* or Kosinski's *Being There,* powerful works dominated by the uncontrolled becoming that the Proteanism of a fragmented culture, supported by a phenomenological perspective, holds out for contemporary man. Henderson's added force foreshadows the powers protagonists in novels by Fowles, Barth, and Durrell will experience when they approach what Durrell calls "reality prime," that is, when they recollect their inner resources, found mirrored in other characters, and thereby begin to make themselves whole.

11 Between Sartre and Freud: Thomas Pynchon's *V.*

In *Seize the Day* and *Henderson the Rain King,* the protagonists develop by interacting with men or other living creatures. The characters in Thomas Pynchon's *V.,* however, offer a more literal illustration of Sartre's proposition that we are our consciousness of objects. Pynchon's first novel, published in 1963, *V.* is a novel of intentionality, in the sense in which Husserl and Sartre used the word—a novel of individuals with their attention fixed obsessively on objects, most of the objects inanimate or rapidly becoming so. Following Sartre's axiom that one is the consciousness of the objects of one's intention, Pynchon shows us in his collection of focused characters that in being conscious of objects one becomes less and less a consciousness and more and more an object. This is the negative side of the Sartrean and American freedom that allows us to become something different by a simple shift of attention.

In *V.* the four major characters are Benny Profane, Herbert Stencil, Fausto Maijstral, and the woman whose original name is probably Victoria Wrenn (Reine?).[1] If we put the most ambivalent of these, Profane, and the most complex, Fausto, aside for the moment, we can see the Sartrean pattern very clearly in the other two. Victoria, between 1898 when we first meet her and 1943 when she dies, becomes increasingly focused on pieces of virtu, little objets d'art. Herbert, between 1945 when he awakens from the sleepwalk in which he spent his

1. Christine N. Cowan brought the possible significance of this name to my attention.

first forty-five years and 1956 when we last see him, fixes his attention solely upon V. and so becomes whatever it or she becomes. The pattern of the novel would be that simple except that, for a reason we have ultimately to infer, Profane perversely refuses to focus his attention completely on the objects that most interest him, attractive young women. He generally approaches, then avoids them. In that perversity lies a disturbing dissonance that alerts us to the minotaur hidden at the center of Pynchon's otherwise simple labyrinth. The complexity of Fausto's relationship with his island Malta provides an alternative to the Sartrean pattern that dominates the other characters.

For *V.* is a novel of objects and of people becoming objects, as the early reviewers were quick to notice.[2] The majority of the characters, major and minor, know what objects are vital to their sense of identity. The catalog is immense and delightfully absurd. Da Conho, the mad Brazilian Zionist salad man at Schlozhauer's Trocadero, lavishes attention on the .30-caliber machine gun with which he longs to defend some still-unidentified kibbutz, a hemisphere away, against Arabs.[3] Rachel Owlglass, who early in the story makes love to her MG (28–29), later directs her mothering love toward the victims of New York, whom she pities in an impersonally abstract manner (358–59). Rachel's favorite victim, Esther Harvitz, becomes almost rocklike in her pursuit of the ideal nose (48, 110). Esther's plastic surgeon, Dr. Schoenmaker, uses a platonically abstract ideal of soulful beauty to excuse his sexual, financial, and physical abuse of her (296–97). Another artist, the painter Slab, follows Schoenmaker by focusing, in his own revolt against his earlier Catatonic Expressionism, on the cheese Danish as the obsessive subject of his thirty-five most recent paintings (282). A second doctor, the dentist Dudley Eigenvalue, matches the obsessions of Schoenmaker and Slab with his theory of psychodontia, the hard sciences' answer to Freud's too soft psychoanalysis, and prizes especially a set of dentures containing one ideal upper right canine fashioned from pure titanium (152–53).

Many of Slab's comrades in the Whole Sick Crew focus on elements

2. See, for examples, Walter Slatoff, Review of *V.*, by Thomas Pynchon, in *Epoch*, XII (Spring, 1963), 255–57, and the anonymous review in *Commentary*, XXXVI (Spring, 1963), 258.

3. Thomas Pynchon, *V.* (New York, 1986), 22–23; hereinafter cited parenthetically by page number in the text.

from the New York art world and television. Few, though, are as attached as Fergus Mixolydian, who has become an extension of the television industry by wiring himself to his set (56). The list goes on. In every case, the minor characters in the present episodes are increasingly in danger of taking their identity from the objects or abstractions that obsess them.

A focus on objects may be what one expects of a culture as materialistic as America's is often charged, at least since Ralph Waldo Emerson and Transcendental Idealism, with having become. There is a considerable difference, however, between longing to possess objects and desiring to become them, but this is a difference lost on the characters in *V.*

In the episodes from the past, covering 1898 to 1943, the character once called Victoria shows most clearly the way the tendency to become objects of consciousness has spread. In the earliest of these six brilliant episodes of varying reliability, that set in Egypt, 1898, Victoria has taken an animate object, Goodfellow the British spy, as her central concern (87). Her younger sister Mildred has already succumbed, however, to the nineteenth-century fondness for rocks and fossils (68) and, as the episode proceeds, shifts this fascination to the prosthetic arm of Eric (63) or Hugh (74) Bongo-Shaftesbury, an Egyptologist seemingly in the service of surreptitious German interests in Africa.

Mildred stands in awe when Bongo-Shaftesbury reveals his potency by rolling up his shirt cuff and thrusting "the naked underside of his arm at the girl." What she sees is impressive: "Shiny and black, sewn into the flesh, was a miniature electric switch. . . . Thin silver wires ran from its terminals up the arm, disappearing under the sleeve" (80). These, he explains, lead to his brain. With pride, he calls himself an electromechanical doll (80). And his reason for pride in his electrically enhanced virility becomes clear in the final scene of the chapter when a "flame appears in the area of [his] right hand," followed by another flame, both "brighter orange than the sun," killing Propentine, partner in espionage to Victoria's lover, Goodfellow (94). The whole Egyptian episode foreshadows the development of the book itself, both in its shift from Victoria's romantic intrigue to Mildred's interest in Bongo-Shaftesbury's potency, and in Herbert Stencil's eight impersonations (62), which end in his becoming the impersonal, totally objective vantage point of the final scene (93–94). The novel ends with a parallel expunging of personality from the objective world (492).

Before the book closes, though, Victoria has passed through her own Protean changes, all of them increasingly impersonal. In her second episode, in Florence in 1899, she has replaced Goodfellow with stand-ins, three of them, each an imperfect, mortal surrogate for the sacrificial Christ of the British Empire, in whose cult Victoria now considers herself a nun (167). In addition to this religious abstraction that she uses to license her behavior, she has followed her sister in collecting objects, her first a relic of British imperial sacrifices in Africa, "an ivory comb, five-toothed: whose shape was that of five crucified . . . soldiers of the British Army" killed by Mahdists east of Khartoum in 1883 (167). By the end of the Florence episode, Victoria will add to her collection of British overseas agents Herbert Stencil's father, foreign officer Sidney Stencil, who, we learn much later, was seduced by Victoria "on a leather couch in the Florence consulate" (488), thus creating the germ from which will grow Herbert's quest for V. forty-six years later.

In Florence, corresponding to Victoria's obsession with British agents, other characters have centered their interest on Botticelli's painting of Venus (163–64), on political violence in the cause of abstract liberty (211), or, in the case of Sid Stencil, on a theory of conspiracy as situation that, though abstract, nonetheless generates an animating sense of rapport (188–89). Similarly, young Evan Godolphin is animated by his quest for his father (156).

The elder Godolphin, Hugh, has himself already seen the future. After a lifetime as an explorer, during which he has been repeatedly vivified by quests for the heart of the regions into which his adventures have drawn him, old Hugh has encountered the terror of Vheissu, which is the terror of the twentieth century, the thought of Nothingness. The spider monkeys of Vheissu foreshadow the philosophy of our century; they are all iridescent skin with no soul, all phenomena without noumenon or essence, and are possibly the apelike ancestors of Protean man (170, 204). Between 1883 and 1898, the inhabitants of Vheissu, Hugh has learned, have spread themselves through the tunnel system of the hollow earth from the jungle regions of the earth (168–69) to the Antarctic (204), carrying with them the vision of annihilation, of Nothingness (206). Hugh's vision of Vheissu may be the hallucination of an old man, but it is also the situation that the novel develops until, in the words of young Evan (Herbert's impersonation here), it may become the communion or "anxiety of everyone living in a world none of us wants to see lit into holocaust" (193–94). It is, in fact, the vision toward which Herbert's quest for V. or Victoria is leading him.

After Florence, Victoria surfaces in Paris in 1913, having in the meanwhile plunged into the kingdom of the inanimate. The object of her interest here is Mélanie l'Heuremaudit (roughly meaning "the blackness of the hour is cursed"), a young dancer first sexualized by her father as the passive object of his touch and of a night bird's gaze (394–95). Before meeting Mélanie, Victoria has lost much of her humanity along with her name, which is replaced here by an object, the letter *V.* (410), and the gender label *woman* (404). Through her young lover, her Jarretiére, Victoria enters the world of fetishes. She attempts to use Mélanie with mirrors so as to overcome the lover's age-old problem of submission and dominance. Through mirrors, V. seeks to become a free or transcendent consciousness aware that she is intent upon an object, Mélanie, who is herself a freedom having her lover V.'s free consciousness as her own object (409–10).

In this scene, described by Porcépic (Porky Pigk?), Pynchon gives a keen parody of the difficulty that Sartre considers central to all human interrelationships and thus to the human condition: the longing to become a freedom that has as the object of its intention another freedom of which it is the creator and, at the same time, to be aware of itself both as a freedom creating another freedom and as the object of the beloved's free consciousness. But, for Sartre, V.'s project is doomed, for what V. in love seeks is what lovers generally desire, to become the absolute-being, which would be God.[4] She is doubly doomed because her beloved Mélanie is so nearly an inanimate object. In focusing on Mélanie, V. thus becomes less and less animate.

Because Mélanie draws V. into the kingdom of the inanimate, the Paris, 1913, episode is the novel's richest in clarifying the movement of Victoria's career and the major theme of the book. Here we learn from Porcépic and Itague, the composer and producer, respectively, of the Stravinski-like ballet in which Mélanie will die impaled on a phallic pole (414), that we have been following the cyclical development of a period of cultural decadence. In a very helpful comment, Itague defines a decadence: "[It is] a falling-away from what is human, and the further we fall the less human we become. Because we are less human,

4. Sartre, *Being and Nothingness,* 221–430, esp. 361–79, chiefly 365.

we foist off the humanity we have lost on inanimate objects and abstract theories" (405). He speaks specifically here of the abstract revolution sought by Mikhail Bakunin, Karl Marx, and Vladimir Ulyanov, or Lenin (405).

The novel, however, shows that V. has entered a decadence that swallows all forms of socialism, Marxist and nationalist, left and right, under a single impulse. For Pynchon has visioned history this century, in Eigenvalue's image, as folded cloth with gathers that make it impossible for anyone "situated . . . at the bottom of a fold . . . to determine warp, woof, and pattern anywhere else" (155). At the same time, he has made Victoria a radioactive trace element and fired her through all the folds so that she lights up the pattern of each like a cancer seen on an X-ray screen.

The Paris, 1913, episode gives us the name of the disease: like Victoria, we have become soul-transvestites, "a transvestism not between sexes but between quick and dead, human and fetish" (410). In falling in love with the objects of our virtue, in allowing ourselves to become our consciousness of the objects we value most, we have come to take our essence from the objects, to become like objects, beings without essence. V. has joined a "conspiracy leveled against the animate world" to establish here "a colony of the Kingdom of Death," which is served by the infiltration of "fetish-constructions like V.'s" (411). No longer an explorer seeking the heart of foreign lands like her compatriot and predecessor Hugh Godolphin, she has become a mere tourist content with surfaces, an unthinking traveler who has wandered over the border into the Kingdom of Death, the realm of the inanimate (411). In their narcissistic, voyeuristic act of love, she and Mélanie romantically mimic the act of death. They seek to be "dead at last . . . one with the inanimate universe and with each other." For them, "love play until then . . . becomes an impersonation of the inanimate" (410).

After Paris, V. next appears on Malta in 1919 in the final chapter of the novel. Here her alias is Veronica Manganese (473), a name suggesting the victory not of Wrenns but of an inert chemical. Attended by Evan Godolphin, who is a victim of primitive Great War plastic surgery gone awry, she is no longer content to remain a mere consciousness of objects but is determined to become her objects, her virtu. Modern surgery now assists her "obsession with bodily incorporating little bits of inert matter" (488). One of her eyes has a clock as the iris; her navel is a star sapphire (487–88). She dreams of having "an entire foot . . . of amber and gold, with the veins, perhaps, in intaglio instead of bas-relief . . . a lovely rainbow or wardrobe of different-hued, different-sized and -shaped feet" (488). In short, the descent of Veronica has been direct from the rainbow-skinned monkeys of Vheissu that the elder Godolphin found at the pole. Old Hugh's fear of annihilation, Nothingness, has become the dream that V. pursues (487).

As an emissary from the Kingdom of Death, in the Malta, 1919, episode Veronica stands in deadly contrast to Mara, Maltese for woman (461), the feminine spirit of the island. Once a great goddess of fertility, Mara, abused and outraged by the Turks in 1565 (462), takes her sexual revenge by perverting the sultan's seraglio, where she is held as a concubine. She brags to the sultan: "I have . . . taught your wives to love their own bodies, showed them the luxury of a woman's love; restored potency to your eunuchs so that they may enjoy one another as well as the three hundred perfumed, female beasts of your harem" (463).

On Malta, Veronica, in contrast to Mara, has abandoned her own fertility for the counterurge of political power and has aligned herself with the Italian nationalists and irredentists, including the still-renegade but already combative fascist Benito Mussolini (473, 484). In service to her abstract political cause, she colludes in 1919 with Sidney Stencil, representing British imperial interests as before, to have the indigenous Maltese uprising against British control of the island crushed by a heavy-handed assault of the British navy and the RAF (491). For his service and collusion, Mara sends a waterspout to annihilate Stencil and the three-masted ship, the xebec, in which he leaves the island (492). Veronica goes on to Africa.

In Southwest Africa in 1922, Victoria, now Vera Meroving (236), has begun to look nostalgically backwards. Her companion here, Hedwig Vogelsang (Headwig Birdblood?), mirrors her nostalgia: for both Mildred and Mélanie, whom Victoria last knew at roughly Hedwig's age, "not more than sixteen" (238); for a prosthesis (the wig); and for her earlier family name, Wrenn. With her once again is the old Englishman Hugh Godolphin (241), now totally addled. Vera's own name suggests that, having been an inert chemical on Malta, she has further devolved toward the inanimate by becoming a mere wandering truth. The nature of this abstract truth is suggested by the Merovingian echo in her name, a reminder of melodramatic intrigue, ruthless rivalry, and degraded power. Her new associates, Foppl and Weissmann (playing on "white man" rather than "wise man"), solidly establish the twentieth-century power tradition to which V. belongs. Foppl dreams fondly of the good days from 1904 to 1907, when German imperial power was truly imperial and General Lothar von Trotha was able to put down a revolt of African Hereros and Hottentots with such ruthless power that he eliminated 64,870 of the estimated 80,000 Hereros living in the territory (245). More au courant, Weissmann muses ecstatically about Gabriele D'Annunzio, Mussolini, Italia Irredenta, Fascisti, the National Socialist German Workers' Party, Adolf Hitler from Munich, and politics as "a kind of engineering" with "people as your raw material" (242).

It is von Trotha, however, who has created the model for modern politics, for he has set his followers free to discover the modern pattern in which the man with power and every "black he would henceforth have to kill slid into alignment, assumed a set symmetry, a dancelike poise." For him and for politics thereafter, "It had only to do with the destroyer and the destroyed, and the act which united them, and it had never been that way before" (264). In this new pattern, in which some people are free consciousnesses and others passive objects, one of von Trotha's troopers will put his muzzle against an old woman's head, announce he is going to kill her, and have her look up and masochistically say, "I thank you." Or a seventeen-year-old Herero girl, having been used by the platoon and given a choice between a side-arm and the bayonet, will actually smile, point to both, and, confusing Thanatos with Eros, begin "to shift her hips lazily in the dust" (264).

From the perspective of Victoria, the quest for love that ended disastrously in Paris has, in the Sartrean pattern, now devolved to a point where love gives way to desire and desire gives way to hatred, where the one-time lover, having failed to have the beloved as a pure freedom, desires the beloved as an object to be enjoyed and then blotted out. At this same point, the beloved, having tired of the anguishing freedom of being a pure consciousness, seeks the masochistic calm of being a freedom transcended, an object of the lover's sadistic freedom.[5] This is the sadomasochistic pattern that the spiritual heirs of Foppl's Crew, Manhattan's Whole Sick Crew, especially Slab, Esther, and Rachel, will thirty-four years later know as the "long daisy chain

5. *Ibid.*, 398–404.

of victimizers and victims, screwers and screwees," the way Neuva York seems to be set up (49).

Between Africa in 1922 and New York in 1956, Kurt Mondaugen, a young German engineer already obsessed in the 1922 episode with antennae, will have gone on to Peenemunde to work on Hitler's V-1 and V-2 rockets aimed at London. From Peenemunde he will pass on to Long Island and the American missile industry (227–28), not an uncommon pattern, Pynchon suggests elsewhere, for those who developed German missiles in an age where technology and corporations knew few loyalties beyond the conversion of pure science into money or power.

While Mondaugen returns to Germany, V.'s development takes her back to Malta. Here in 1943, she emerges as both a soul- and a literal transvestite, the Bad Priest, who preaches a sterile abstract philosophy. The Maltese girls she/he advises to "become nuns, avoid the sensual extremes—pleasure of intercourse, pain of childbirth" (341). The boys the Bad Priest tells to be like "the rock of their island," to become "like a crystal: beautiful and soulless" (341). When the Bad Priest dies in a mock crucifixion, the children of Malta find she/he/it comes apart into a wig, an ivory comb, a tattoed scalp, an artificial foot, a star sapphire navel, a set of false teeth, a clockwork eye. In short, she has become the various objects of virtu on which she has fixed her attention (342–43). At the same time, the abstract political cause she has embraced has sent the airplanes and bombs of Mussolini to blast away in "explosive orgasms" at Malta, "a noun feminine and proper," the "womb of rock," who "lies on her back in the sea, sullen; an immemorial woman" (318).

Our witness at the dismantling of V. is Fausto Maijstral, whose "Confessions" we as readers of the novel sample just as Herbert does. Thus the "Confessions" are one of apparently two episodes from the past that have not been transformed by Herbert's obsession with V.; they have not been Stencilized. Their unmediated status is important, for Fausto's account contains a way for human consciousness to deal with objects that is vitally different from Victoria's.

In appearance, Fausto, like Victoria, is Protean, and like her he is preoccupied with objects, but chiefly with one object, the rock of Malta. Fausto distinguishes his own Protean avatars with roman numerals as though they were generations of his descendants. Fausto I was slated to be a priest; Fausto II arrived with the birth of his daughter Paola (306). Fausto III was the product of the world war, of the

Luftwaffe assaults upon his island, especially of the death of Elena, his wife (306, 341), and of his own experience at the disassembling of V. For when he saw V. the Bad Priest begin to cry, Fausto " 'regressed' to the priesthood" he "would have joined" had he not married Elena, and, doing so, he used V.'s own blood as holy oil to administer the sacrament of Extreme Unction. The cold of her lips, however, unlike the cold of the many corpses he handled during the siege of Malta, stayed with him: it was "night's cold, object's cold, nothing human" (344)—a cold therein resembling Fausto III, who comes the closest of all his forms to "non-humanity" (306–307). For "Fausto III [took] on much of the non-humanity of the debris, crushed stone, broken masonry, destroyed churches and auberges of his city" (307).

V. ends as debris. Fausto III's devolution bottoms out, then turns a curve, and he begins "his slow return to consciousness or humanity" as Fausto IV, the man of letters, the author of poems, monographs, and critical essays (307). The key to Fausto's survival and renewed humanity seems to be that, in contrast to V., who, like a chameleon taking its color from its surroundings, increasingly took things into herself, he, in the traditional way of the poet and Narcissus, puts himself into things, colors his surroundings with his original humanity, invests himself heavily in the landscape of his island. Consequently, when the war ends, he can withdraw his investment and reclaim his humanity. His landscape is a rock, but to the benefit of Fausto and the Maltese people, it is also an "inviolable womb" (318), or that, at least, is the way their metaphors, guided by Fausto, shape the island. Metaphors here are of the essence: they are the way a poet or a people invest their humanity in the objects around them, humanize the external world, and populate the otherwise uninhabited streets and landscapes of the twentieth century with living creatures like themselves (323–24).

For Fausto, even a population of "ghosts, monsters, criminals, deviates," primitive bugaboos of the participation mystique that Lucien Lévy-Bruhl describes, seems preferable to the soulless masses and shadows that a world devoid of human coloration has left the century heir to (324). He writes to his daughter: "The same motives which cause us to populate a dream-street also cause us to apply to a rock [Malta] human qualities like 'invincibility,' 'tenacity,' 'perseverance,' etc. More than metaphor, it is delusion. But on the strength of this delusion Malta survived. . . . Manhood on Malta thus became increasingly defined in terms of rockhood" (325). Like Winston Churchill showing his famous V to give the British people a vision of victory, Fausto goes about his island playing "the 'role' of the poet, this 20th Century." That role, he says, is to lie (326).

But Fausto's is lying of the most profound sort, he contends, the kind "poets have been at . . . for centuries," their service to society, without which society "would live no longer than the quick memories and dead books of their poetry" (326). Painfully aware that no metaphor has validity beyond its function or is ever more than "a device, an artifice," Fausto continues to cloak the "innate mindlessness" of the "universe of things which simply are" with "comfortable and pious metaphor so that the 'practical' half of humanity may continue in the Great Lie," believing that the things about them—such things as "machines, dwellings, streets and weather"—all "share the same human motives, personal traits and fits of contrariness as they" (326).

Fausto's form of poetic narcissism has significance beyond Malta's survival. As Melville warns us in the first chapter of *Moby-Dick,* the myth of Narcissus tormented by the image of himself in the fountain "is the key to it all."[6] The practical half of humanity, Fausto explains, "may look on the laws of physics as legislation and God as a human form with beard measured in light-years and nebulae for sandals." Fausto's kind, however, poets like Melville and himself, know that our sciences and religions, too, are but metaphors used to lend human qualities to the mindless universe (326). This insight, at once deflating and ennobling, has been approached by some modern scientists in their discipline's less grandiose moments, most notably by the English astronomer, physicist, mathematician, and expositor of relativity theory, Arthur Stanley Eddington, when he called his scientific epistemology "selective subjectivism."

If Great Lies or Life Lies or mythologies carry the dangers of fanaticism and eventual disillusionment, these risks seem to be less for Fausto, especially in our time, than the contrary myth pursued by V., that we are our consciousness of objects. Especially is fanaticism the lesser danger for a poet like Fausto, who is "always acutely conscious" that the value of metaphor is totally functional rather than intrinsic,

6. Herman Melville, *Moby-Dick; or, The Whale,* ed. Alfred Kazin (Boston, 1956), 24.

that the metaphorical qualities (invincibility, tenacity, perseverance, and so on) ultimately belong to the mind that beholds them, not to the world to which they are ascribed. Knowing thus that metaphor is noble narcissism, the poet has the power to lead in the eventual reclamation of those human qualities that have been invested in the outer world for safekeeping. In this upward phase of the cycle, Fausto, like the people of Malta, reclaims his human traits from the womb of rock and is reborn as Fausto IV, thus avoiding the fate of (a Fausto) V.

It is especially important that Fausto's confessions have not passed through the transforming medium of Herbert's imagination. Only so could Fausto's special relation to the objects of the world have escaped contamination by Herbert's own manner of treating objects, which is not narcissistic but chameleonlike in that Herbert becomes what he is conscious of rather than transforms the outer world with metaphors of his own humanity. The distinction here is a subtle one and not absolute. The woman V. that we as readers see in four of the six episodes from the past has been contaminated by Herbert's needs and fears. The V. of these episodes could be Herbert's invention altogether, except for the initial taken from his father's Florence, 1899, journal (53–54). Her transformation into objects of her consciousness, therefore, could be Herbert's habit of thinking rather than hers. But Fausto's confessions and apparently the final chapter, Malta, 1919, have escaped the prism of Herbert's mind. Because V. in these two un-Stencilized episodes is clearly as obsessed with becoming objects as she/he/it is in the episodes filtered through Herbert, the paradox of the chicken and egg does not apply. The pattern of causality is reasonably clear: it runs from V. as cause to Herbert as imitation.

V., however, is not the first cause. She herself reflects the historical movement of the century. Whether we start with Husserl's logic, Darwin's fossils, or Marx's labor-value theories; with late industrial society or consumer culture as described by Thorstein Veblen; with D'Annunzio, Mussolini, von Trotha, or Hitler in Munich; or with Vheissu, the direction this century has taken is the same: toward less humanity and more objectification, even objectification of people, who in this way become the walking inanimate. Although it is finally impossible to say whether the contrast between the decline of other major figures and Fausto's renewal suggests an element of free choice or merely that Fausto grew up in a different environment, it is clear that Malta, for all its turmoil, provided him with a traditional culture from which to select his roles, including that of poet.

Nor does the career of Herbert Stencil ascribe to free choice a primary role in determining whether a character uses the environment for creative mirroring or for passive modeling. Herbert begins in a somnambulant state, and his pursuit of V. animates his life. Before V., he was only half-conscious, slothful; he was a sleepwalker knocking about Europe and Africa, freeloading on his dead father's former acquaintances, picking up odd jobs, working in troubled times for the British Foreign Office in the usual "fuzzily defined spy/interpreter/liaison capacity" of would-be adventurers (54–55). In short, he appears as though out of the pages of an early poem by T. S. Eliot: one of the many that death has undone, another Prufrock, a hollow man, one of the denizens of London walking about in a ring, a modernist zombie without traditions or direction.

The causes given for his suspended state, though, are more personal than cultural. Born in 1901, Herbert grew up with his father away on business and a mother whose total absence was never explained: "Died in childbirth, ran off with someone, committed suicide: some way of vanishing painful enough to keep Sidney from ever referring to it" (52). We can reconstruct the importance of these absences for Herbert from his spending much of his first forty-four years studying his father's journals for names of old friends he might ask to lend him a helping hand and the next eleven years pursuing the mysterious V. mentioned in one entry, a woman who, before the question is even asked, he emphatically denies could be his mother (54). In fact, even though Victoria could be his biological mother, the chronology we are given, the April, 1899, seduction and the May, 1901, birth, seems to rule it out. (Sidney's own music-hall ditty about Herbert's birth, in which the mother "would stay to home / 'Er 'eart all filled wiv pain" because Sidney was "down to the pub again" (466), gives a picture of the mother that would not fit the V. we see either before or after 1901. Although this song probably should not be taken too seriously, it raises at least a ghost of a possibility that Herbert's father was not Sidney but the ubiquitous milkman of domestic male paranoia.) If not his biological mother, V. between 1945 and 1956 is clearly his psychological mother, and the degree of her influence measures the depth of his longing for the missing maternal force.

His need for a mothering influence increased during World War II, which he spent in North Africa (later the setting in which he imagines Victoria Wrenn's encounter with Goodfellow). By the end of the war he has "seen more dead than he cared to again" and is flirting "with the idea of resuming [the] prewar sleepwalk," when the sentences about V. in his father's journal for the first time speak to him (54). The shock and the search that follow deliver him "from inertness to—if not vitality, then at least activity," to "work, the chase—for it was V. he hunted" (55).

The pleasure of his work is narcissistic, but not in the noble sense of Fausto's poetic work. In fact, it is not really V. that Herbert pursues but the maintenance of the energy she creates in him, for "what love there was to Stencil had become directed entirely inward, toward this acquired sense of animateness" (55). Consequently, like Benny Profane pursuing girls, he cannot psychologically afford to achieve his quest. Finding V. would end the inward animation he values. Like Benny, he must "approach and avoid" (55).

Once his pursuit begins, he sacrifices his inwardness to the process that enables him to discover, or invent, V.'s past. He calls his technique "forcible dislocation of personality" (62). It is his habit of "always [referring] to himself in the third person" (62), of keeping himself open for his impersonation of the point-of-view characters who allow him to slip into V.'s story. Both the power and the danger of his novelistlike habit appear in the Egypt, 1898, chapter, the first of the past episodes. Here Herbert invents V.'s adventures from eight points of view: he impersonates seven minor characters, P. Aieul, café waiter and amateur libertine (63); Yusef the factotum (66); Maxwell Rowley-Bugge, vaudevillean and abuser of young Alices (69–70); Waldetar the conductor (77); Gebrail the cabman (83); Girgis the mountebank (85); Hanne the Bavarian barmaid (88), and then *becomes* the purely objective vantage point in the final part of the Egyptian chapter (94).

At the level of comedy, this tour de force constitutes a brilliant parody of the Joycean, modernist novel with its scrupulous documentation of point of view, a process honoring twentieth-century discoveries concerning the relativity of knowledge. At another level, it is a breakthrough, comparable to what Durrell achieved in *Balthazar* in 1958, from the modernist technique in fiction to the postmodern. The chapter title tells us that Herbert's presence should be felt in each of the points of view and that the episode is not dramatic in the Jamesian or

Joycean sense but is actually first-person omniscient, like all fiction, no matter how realistic and dramatic it may pretend to be.

At the thematic level, however, the final section of the episode foreshadows the fate of Herbert and the vision of the novel. Here Herbert's pursuit of V. transforms him into pure consciousness of the events described, the purely objective vantage from which, like the final page of the novel, all human personality has been expunged. Sadly, in his pursuit of objective knowledge, Herbert, who began with immense powers of human phantasy and imagination capable of first-person omniscience, ends by expunging himself from the episode.

For the second of the episodes from V.'s life, Florence, 1899, Herbert regains a degree of humanity by impersonating Evan Godolphin (156). As Evan, he shares in the young man's animating pursuit of his once-dynamic father, Hugh. But before the Florence episode, we already know something of Evan's fate, that in the Great War he will become a pilot in the RAF, be shot up in the battle of Meuse-Argonne, have his face horribly disfigured, and then become the victim of a young doctor named Halidom who "favored allografts: the introduction of inert substances into the living face" (98–99). Evan's perfectly reconstructed face within six months will decompose, the result of "foreign-body reaction," the body's natural defense against the invasion of unfamiliar substances (100). This is the same Evan who will reappear on Malta in 1919 as V.'s protector and caretaker, his face now "too grotesque, too deliberately, preciously Gothic to be real," the nose and chin and eye all malformed or inanimate (475–76). Even in Florence, 1899, Herbert as Evan further fragments himself into multiple consciousnesses to become the minor conspirators Mantissa, the Machiavellian Fox; Gaucho, the bomb-tossing Lion; and Cesare, the seedy Pig (159).

The next episode Herbert collects from the past is the account of Southwest Africa in 1922. For this story he relies on the engineer Kurt Mondaugen, formerly of Peenemunde, currently of Long Island's Yoyodyne, Inc. and American missiles (227). As a participant in the events of 1922, Mondaugen seems more reliable than Herbert's earlier sources, his father's enigmatic journals and his own imagination. Before the dentist Eigenvalue and the reader can hear of the events in Africa, however, Herbert turns Mondaugen's thirty-minute yarn into a fifty-one-page chapter (229–79). It has "undergone considerable change: had become, as Eigenvalue put it, Stencilized" (228, *cf.* 249).

Here Herbert, as he retells the story, impersonates Mondaugen, a vital detail that helps justify Hugh Godolphin's confusing Mondaugen with his son Evan (253), whom Herbert impersonated in the Florence episode.

Because Mondaugen is largely Herbert, the chief problem ascribed to Mondaugen in this most dreamlike and surreal of all the episodes should be reascribed to Herbert himself. That problem is the difficulty of finding a source for the collective dream of decadence and sadism that dominates life in the Southwest Protectorate. Herbert merged with Mondaugen says: "If dreams are only waking sensation first stored and later operated on, then the dreams of a voyeur [*i.e.*, one who is consciousness of the objects he sees] can never be his own. . . . He'd no idea, for instance, where this had come from" (254–55). As a consequence, in the common dream of *herrenschaft,* or German rule, and the cultural inferiority of Africa, Mondaugen blurs dream and reality along with values and characters (255), much the way Herbert blurs the boundaries between himself and the various persons he has impersonated. As have the voyeur's, Herbert's dreams and his personality have become less and less his own.

On the positive side, Herbert's slipping into the common dream of the century, his learning to conspire (breathe together) with his contemporaries, carries him toward the cosmic symmetry of the age, the pattern of destroyer and destroyed, the Dance of Death (264, 296). On the negative side, however, his impersonations, when he reflects on them, make him suspect that he is undergoing his own form of soul-transvestism, that he has lost his individual self and become something abstract, "purely the century's man," "contemporary man in search of an identity," "quite purely He Who Looks for V." (226), in short, a pure consciousness of the object V. He recognizes that V. is part of "the Big One, the century's master cabal," or "the ultimate Plot Which Has No Name" (226). He does not realize, however, that his means of pursuing her, his forcible dislocations of personality, have turned him into another soul-transvestite and, like V., a victim of the ultimate plot of the century and the plot of the novel, to the degree that the book finally has a plot.

Because Herbert receives his next information about V., the confessions of Fausto Maijstral, directly and Pynchon passes it on to the reader before Herbert has an opportunity to edit or contaminate it, we as readers here have an opportunity to contrast Herbert's thought processes to Fausto's as we did Fausto's to V.'s. Both men are authors and Protean, but in very different ways. Fausto's confessions, for example, are of necessity autobiographical; throughout his changes (306–307), he remains Fausto in relation to his changing world. His world shapes him, but his essential Fausto identity survives the external influences. Herbert's fictions, on the other hand, are totally dramatic; Herbert loses himself in the characters he impersonates, even though his needs (for a father and a mother) and fears (of increasing dehumanization) show through the personae.

One could argue that Herbert is a more daring, even better creator than Fausto, but Fausto is a better reader of what he creates. Whereas Herbert becomes his characters and what they are conscious of, Fausto knows that his characters, especially Malta the womb of rock, are metaphors, projections of human qualities that originate in himself. Both men succeed in reading themselves into their creations. Only Fausto knows how to read himself out of his creations, how to reclaim his projections that animate the external world as resources rightly belonging to him, not to the world around him (325–26). For Herbert, the terrifying conspiracies remain in the outer world. He is not able to read them as, in part at least, the mirror of his own fear. The process of dehumanization is a real-world event; as the greater reliability of the confessions relative to the earlier episodes from V.'s career proves, the conspiracy against the animate is not altogether the product of Herbert's paranoia. Herbert's failure to reclaim the needs and fears he has projected, though, robs him of his inner self, his essential resource, and thereby swamps him in the process he finds so ominous.

After the "Confessions," Herbert's next report of V., which he recounts to Benny in 1956 (392), came originally from Porcépic, V.'s confidant in Paris, 1913 (409, 412). The detailed descriptions of the permutations and combinations of transvestism and sexual roles attempted by V. and Mélanie very probably were in what Porcépic was told by V. herself and years later repeated to Herbert (409), but the episode has once again been Stencilized. It is therefore probable that the terrifying speculations about V.'s "progression toward inanimateness," transvestism between quick and dead, and the "establishment here of a colony of the Kingdom of Death" (411) are in large part the product of Herbert's habit of thinking. Stencil's presence is strong in the pages that contain these speculations (406–12), including the opinion held in the Rusty Spoon (where the Whole Sick Crew hang out) "that Stencil was seeking in [V.] his own identity" (411).

In a story of 1956 or a novel of 1963, a character seeking his own identity is cliché enough to pass as satire. Here, though, the reference turns up in the sentence preceding the description of V.'s fetishism as an infiltration of the Kingdom of Death (411). Knowing all that we know through him, we can see that were Herbert a better reader, that is, less a phenomenologist and more willing to acknowledge the unconscious as one's own being separate from one's self-knowledge, he would be able to make the essential connection, see the nature of the identity he is seeking, abrogate his quest for V., and thus stay off Malta. But Herbert believes that he is what he is conscious of, his pursuit of V., and that the quest is what animates him. Therefore he represses his longstanding apprehension about Malta, on which he thinks his father died (303), and goes to the island "like a nervous groom to matrimony," a marriage that Herbert imagines was "arranged by Fortune" (389). In attributing his motive here to Fortune, a force in the external world, he again denies the energy working in his own unacknowledged unconscious.

On Malta the ominous nature of Herbert's quest finally works its way into his consciousness, and this is the moment of highest recognition in the novel, the *anagnorisis* of Herbert's bittersweet but tragic quest. The moment is as subtle as a recognition scene in a late novel by Henry James; for the reader's understanding what is revealed presumes that he carry in mind the major events and themes of the novel, even events that on the surface are sufficiently unlike one another to rule out effective association.

The recognition occurs when Stencil learns from Father Avalanche that the latter's predecessor on Malta was a Father Fairing, who went to America (449). For reasons no one explains, Herbert, his pulse jumping, his breathing out of control, leaves the old priest and tries to walk himself back into self-control, thinking as he goes that this detail "clinches it"—clinches something that again goes unexplained. Back at his quarters, his mind reeling with questions of coincidence and Providence, paranoia and appalling conspiracies, Herbert mentions Father Fairing to his fellow traveler, Benny Profane. Profane, half to himself, wonders whether it is "the same Father Fairing" and recounts one of his adventures on the Alligator Patrol in the New York sewers, "how he'd hunted one pinto beast through Fairing's Parish; cornered and killed it in a chamber lit by some frightening radiance" (450). Again Herbert is too appalled to speak but manages, with as much control as he can muster, his retreat to Fausto's house to report that Profane "has a soul possessed by the devil" and is sleeping in Herbert's own bed (450). What Herbert means is that he was himself shot in Father Fairing's parish (451), the New York sewers (117), where his search for V. once caused him to don a waterproof suit and diving mask, gear so deforming his appearance that Profane, in the strange phosphorescent light below the street, mistook him for an alligator (122–23).

Once again, on Malta, Herbert is in Fairing's parish. Again there is a strange light, which he takes to be the presence, perhaps the soul, of V. (447). And again there is Profane, whom Herbert entrapped into coming along for the ride. To Stencil's way of thinking, the configuration is the same. It is perfect and so clinches his worst suspicion, that "events seem to be ordered into an ominous logic," accent any phrase he may choose (449). The streets of the twentieth century are haunted by emissaries from the same cabal, all members of one conspiracy (450). They are out to kill Herbert, and Profane, his body possessed by V., is the devil they have sent to do it (450).

But Fausto, the wiser reader, responds to Herbert's now-boundless paranoia with humor—sardonic but therapeutic humor. Fausto first refuses Herbert's request for an exorcist to drive the devils from Herbert's life: "One would have to exorcise the city, the island, every ship's crew on that Mediterranean. The continents, the world. Or the western part. . . . We are western men" (451). Fausto implies here that as Western men we have no cultural way of understanding the psychological reality of myth. He goes on to make light of Herbert's conspiratorial thinking by ironically confirming the blackest of all twentieth-century historical paranoias, the fraudulent Zionist conspiracy: "Yes, yes. Thirteen of us rule the world in secret" (451). This self-evident exaggeration pushes Herbert to his moment of deepest self-understanding. He asks Fausto and himself, "Is it really his own extermination he's after?" (451).

In raising the possibility that he pursues V. to bring about his own death, Herbert hovers above the insight that makes sense of most of the events in the novel: that he and the others who represent the century are driven by Thanatos, the death instinct; that the pursuit of an identity limited to consciousness of objects leads to becoming the objects one is conscious of; that this condition is a form of soul-transvestism in which the quick swap essences with dead things. Fausto gives him the clue he needs to read this drive toward self-extermination from the story of his pursuit. Fausto answers his question about self-destruction with "Ask her. . . . Ask the rock" (451). In other words, Fausto tells him to distinguish human metaphor ("her") from inanimate rock in order to reclaim, in Itague's earlier language, his own lost humanity foisted off "on inanimate objects and abstract theories" (405), in his case the abstract quest for V.

Rather than turn from the abstractness of modern philosophy to an insight of modern psychology, Herbert turns, as John W. Hunt perceived twenty years ago, to the evasions of misology. The essential insight about himself, V., and the age is so dark, so much to be feared and hated, that he rejects the vision toward which he and the novel have been building: he rejects his own plot and that of the book. To keep his quest, his feeling of inward animation, from ending, he clutches at a clue about V.'s glass eye and takes a boat leaving Malta (451–52), thinking thereby to avoid his father's fate.

What Herbert does not know and what we, not Herbert, learn in the final, seemingly un-Stencilized chapter is that his father died not on Malta but on a boat leaving Malta (492). In short, in abrogating the insight toward which he has been moving, Herbert unwittingly follows again in his dead father's footsteps (or wake) and so ends his quest by finding what he has been seeking. The thrust of the novel is that he will overtake the death he searches for *off* Malta. Such, it appears, is the fate of those who pursue the past through the twentieth century into the kingdom of the inanimate.

With Herbert's fate as a backdrop, Benny Profane's ambivalence is easier to comprehend. His schlemiellike hesitation, his uncertainty about how to act, seems the better part of wisdom. Profane has a keen intuition that the two dimensions of the characters here, the obsession with objects and the death drive, are somehow linked. His actions from the beginning warn the reader that things are not quite right in mid-twentieth-century America.

Profane focuses on seemingly animate beings, young women such as Rachel, Josefina, and Paola. But even the best of these, he fears, if they are not already smitten by their love for machines, if they are not already the young Victorias of a modern generation, have convex heels and lie back and take it from objects like any inanimate thing (288). This passive quality, which Benny as a schlemiel fears he shares, is what he dreads; so he spends much of the novel saying no to appealing young women (145, 378). The turning point comes when Benny, whose mother's absence was filled by too much "inanimate food" (379–80), allows Rachel Owlglass, who thinks she must mother homeless victims (358–59), to con him. She uses her crotch as an object that "when it talks we listen" (384) to get Benny to forget his fear of mechanical women and make love to her (385).

Ultimately, on Malta he meets Brenda Wigglesworth, who owns seventy-two pairs of Bermuda shorts (452). She is his dame of doom. With her, it becomes clear that the determinism of the inanimate has caught even Profane. He is last seen running with Brenda down the intersecting vectors of the streets of Valletta, "through the abruptly absolute night . . . toward the edge of Malta, and the Mediterranean beyond," the domain of Mara, where Sidney and apparently Sidney's son both went down (455).

Profane and Herbert live in a culture where people in bars talk "proper nouns" (131) and where, as part of a line, a boy will ask a girl, "What do you think of Sartre's thesis that we are all impersonating an identity?" (130). In the mid-1950s, the slogans of Sartre and the assumptions of phenomenology are the background against which both the mating rituals and the artistic, intellectual life of the Western world, even in America, are conducted. Phenomenology is an almost invisible element of the air that Profane, Herbert, and the other contemporary characters breathe. It came out of much the same European background as Victoria Wrenn did, was tempered in the same political fires, thrived with her. By the mid-1950s, V. has become little more than a presence, a light, that Herbert feels in Valletta (447). The popularity of Sartre has established phenomenology, however, as the medium through which multitudes view themselves and their world, even though those who do so do not use Husserl's word, because the word *existentialism* is recondite enough to conjure with.

Before Herbert dies, he has begun to discover that one may live consciously in the phenomenological world of Husserl, Sartre, and existentialism and still dwell unconsciously in the psychological world of

Freud. Phenomenology, by valuing pure transcendental consciousness so highly, may significantly affect the nature of the unconscious, for the unconscious, when denied, has to compensate for the etiolated conscious life. By focusing solely on phenomena outside himself, Herbert has, without knowing it, given himself over to Thanatos, the death drive, the more destructive of the major principles discussed by Freud, rather than to Eros. To Freud, after the horrors of the Great War, the organic instincts in humankind appeared exceedingly conservative; the "final goal of all organic striving" seemed to be to restore "an *old* state of things, an initial state from which the living entity has at one time or other departed and to which it is striving to return by the circuitous paths along which its development leads." Because "*inanimate things existed before living ones,*" everything living seeks to become "inorganic once again." The "*aim of all life is death.*"[7] This is the knowledge that Herbert seeks to ignore by leaving Malta. Viewed from the double perspectives of Sartre and Freud, the surface of *V.* is redundantly and convincingly phenomenological, but its deep structure, though denied, remains ominously psychological.

Husserl plays a special role in all this, for we generally look to our philosophers for clues regarding the nature of our being. But Husserl's delight in abstract truth and pure objective logic so blurred the line between epistemology and ontology that our civilization once more (as it often has since Plato) confused what we think with what we are, knowledge with being. Seeking to become Husserl's pure transcendental ego or Sartre's pure consciousness, we neglect or ignore the levels of our being that remain mysteries outside consciousness. In *V.*, the phenomenological emphasis on the transcendental ego and consciousness of objects becomes itself a form of bad faith or repression. It leads the characters to project, to foist off, the denied psychological unconscious onto objects and abstractions that become increasingly fascinating the more one denies the unconscious. Ultimately, Pynchon's people endow such objects with enough attraction to dominate the characters' lives and destroy them.

As Freud discovered and Pynchon shows, the repressed always returns, in this case through objects and abstractions whose borrowed

7. Sigmund Freud, *Beyond the Pleasure Principle,* trans. James Strachey (New York, 1959), 70–71, emphasis in original; *cf.* Sigmund Freud, *Civilization and Its Discontents,* ed. and trans. James Strachey (New York, 1961), 65–66.

"personality" actually belongs to the characters.[8] More often than anyone cares to admit, we fail to see things as they are but instead see them as we are. Unable to reclaim our own human quality, Narcissus-like we long to embrace the phantom of life and, like V., Sidney, Herbert, Benny, and Captain Ahab before them, go down again into the mindless voids of the universe of things. In tracing this path, Pynchon raises the probability that philosophy during the first half of the twentieth century, unwittingly and through an ominous logic, placed itself in the service of Thanatos.

8. Sigmund Freud, "Repression," in *A General Selection from the Works of Sigmund Freud*, ed. John Rickman (Garden City, N.Y., 1957), 92.

III Reclaiming the Core: John Fowles's *The Magus*

In *V.,* because talk of Sartre fills the air and characters are engrossed by the objects surrounding them, individuals become existentialists largely by blind habit. In contrast, the protagonist of *The Magus,* John Fowles's second novel, published in 1965, *elects* to become an existentialist during his university days, but his decision arises largely because existentialism is a fad. In his existential phase, Fowles's protagonist treats the women with whom he has affairs as though they are objects of consciousness. The novel, however, dramatizes the consequence of his encountering two women who will not allow him to treat them in this fashion.

When Fowles dismisses *The Magus* as a failure, partially because of its adolescent longing for "an experience beyond the literary," he is being too modest.[1] The novel's immense popularity (5), I would argue, rather than deriving from a weakness, has to do with its narrative purity: it is the richest narrative in his canon in part because it does less than others of his novels to explain itself. In allowing the story to speak for itself, Fowles creates a major character who defies being understood from a single psychological perspective. The character's psychological complexity thus makes multiple interpretations possible and generates new readings. It also challenges the flexibility of individ-

1. John Fowles, *The Magus: A Revised Version* (Boston, 1977), 6; hereinafter cited parenthetically by page number in the text. References to the original version will be cited parenthetically in text as *Mg* plus page number.

ual psychological theories. What I propose to do, without attempting to exhaust the meanings of the novel, is to bring a variety of psychological approaches to bear on the central character, Nicholas Urfe.

In doing so, I will blend theories of Freud, whom the novel indicates Fowles knew a good deal about; Jung, among whose admirers Fowles counted himself at the time (6); and Heinz Kohut, the Freudian revisionist, whose contributions Fowles almost certainly could not have known in the early 1960s.[2] Only through multiple approaches like these can we begin to understand the problem that wrecks all of Nicholas' relationships with women, explore the causes that underlie his malaise, and determine the effectiveness of the mythic masque, or psychodrama, that Maurice Conchis, the magus, stages to lead him out of his confusion.

No other sentence in the novel better describes the nature of Nicholas' basic problem than his own early comment: "In our age it is not sex that raises its ugly head, but love" (34). He is thinking of his own affair with Alison, specifically of the manner in which it began as a simple leap into bed but then grew complicated as tenderer emotions emerged between them. He has in mind the period when, even in museums, he experienced sudden moments of feeling that they were "one body, one person," when he felt "that if she had disappeared it would have been as if [he] had lost half of [him]self" (35). Against this tenderness his only defense is to drive "her straight home and [tear] her clothes off" (35). He is reacting here to a perceived doubleness in Alison that he finds intolerable. In his first view of her, for example, he notes that she is "waif-like, yet perversely or immorally so" (23), that she has "two voices; one almost Australian, one almost English" (23),

2. When Jung writes that Freud and he "were in complete agreement" that "the main problem of medical psychotherapy is the *transference,*" in C. G. Jung, *Memories, Dreams, Reflections,* ed. Aniela Jaffé (New York, 1965), 212, he establishes the common ground I am building upon; for my study works with the expanded form of transference Jungians call "projection," in which a wider range of unconscious materials than Freud had in mind (chiefly unfinished business with parents and siblings for Freud) is transferred to carriers other than the analyst. Regarding the unity of Freud and Kohut, Robert S. Wallerstein, in "Self Psychology and 'Classical' Psychoanalytical Psychology: The Nature of Their Relationship," in *The Future of Psychoanalysis,* ed. Arnold Goldberg (New York, 1983), 27, 58–60, argues persuasively that both psychoanalysts were working within the unifying paradigm of psychoanalysis.

and that her "candid grey eyes [are] the only innocent things in a corrupt face" (24). Because he finds her a bizarre "kind of human oxymoron" (24) who can call herself "a whore and a colonial" and yet inspire a closeness in him that leads them to talk of marriage (35) and children (34), Nicholas eventually feels driven to abandon her, the way he has at least "a dozen girls" (21), and to make his escape to Greece.

Using traditional language, one would say that Nicholas makes a strict distinction between ideal and sexual love, that he insists on separating Artemis from Aphrodite, that he divides the women he knows into the pale and the dark (319), Madonnas and Whores, and that these are absolute categories permitting no middle ground. Because Alison in some bizarre fashion blends the two types, she so overwhelms his masculine categories of defense that he has no other option except to run from the confusion she causes. In the twentieth century, with the help of one of Freud's key essays on sexuality, "The Most Prevalent Form of Degradation in Erotic Life," written in 1912, one can say a good deal more about the form of "psychical impotence" that governs Nicholas' behavior before he becomes part of the masquelike experiment Maurice Conchis conducts on the island of Phraxos.

From Freud's perspective, Nicholas behaves repeatedly like one of those men who have no desire for the women they love and no love for the women they desire, except that, for reasons we will examine below, Nicholas has not yet found where he loves and so pretends "that there [is] nowhere to love" (17). For Freud, "a fully normal attitude in love" must unite "two currents of feeling," both "the tender, affectionate feelings and the sensual feelings." Although Nicholas is obviously not "totally impotent" by Freud's definition, according to which "the whole amount of sensual feeling" conceals "itself behind the tender feelings," he seems to suffer from the less severe condition in which the sensual feeling remains "sufficiently strong and unchecked to secure some outlet for itself in reality" but "above all" must avoid "all association with feelings of tenderness." Freud explains: "The sensual feeling that has remained active seeks only objects evoking no reminder of the incestuous persons [the mother or sister] forbidden to it; the impression made by someone who seems deserving of high estimation leads, not to sensual excitation, but to feelings of tenderness which remain erotically ineffectual. The erotic life of such people remains dissociated. . . . In order to keep their sensuality out of contact with the objects they love, they seek out objects whom they need not love."[3] The pattern of all Nicholas' romances before Alison has consisted of such scrupulous avoidance of tender emotions for the girls with whom he has slept.

Alison perforce falls prey to the pattern simply because, as their relationship progresses, she becomes increasingly loving and lovable and thereby necessarily less desirable, as Nicholas understands desire. Freud's description perfectly fits the young man: "The strange refusal implied in psychical impotence is made whenever the [desired] objects selected in order to avoid incest possess some trait, often quite inconspicuous, reminiscent of the objects [the mother or sister] that must be avoided."[4] Because Alison possesses an unusually fine capacity for loving, her relationship with Nicholas is doomed from the start.

All of Nicholas' affairs are similarly doomed, for the "line" he uses causes him unwittingly to attract women with the doubleness he finds unacceptable: "My 'technique' was to make a show of unpredictability, cynicism, and indifference" (21). His approach draws to him women with a matching disposition, ready to jump into bed for the shock of the moment, to ask few questions, and to expect very little afterward. This is the side of Nicholas that attracts the side Alison has developed to deal with men like Nicholas or her Australian boyfriend Pete—the side of Alison that can tell Nicholas, "I'm going to be a stupid Australian slut for ever" (29). Like Alison, though, Nicholas has an unmanageable doubleness of his own. For, as he tells us, first he shows a woman his cad side; "then, like a conjurer with his white rabbit," he produces "the solitary heart" (21). As a result, the women who find him attractive must possess, in addition to the cynical, easy-sex exterior that initially engages a man psychically potent enough to tolerate only the sensual dimension of a woman, a strong maternal side capable of tender feelings. Although Nicholas takes pride in his ability to collect and unload women (21), he seems totally unconscious of the way his own doubleness booby-traps all his relationships.

He considers his avoidance of tenderness an existential assumption of "responsibility with my total being" (21). At this point in his life, he fancies himself an existentialist in the French mode: he sees himself as

3. Sigmund Freud, "Contributions to the Psychology of Love: The Most Prevalent Form of Degradation in Erotic Life," in Freud, *Collected Papers,* ed. Joan Riviere (4 vols.; London, 1934), IV, 204, 207.

4. *Ibid.,* 207.

a blend of "wartime aesthete and cynic" in combination with a post-war, capricious, selfish young man in revolt. This existentialist he takes to be his "real self" (16–17). By identifying with such fads, chiefly because they would have shocked his now-dead parents, he has become nothing except a mask; and even in revolt against his father he is "still no less under his influence" (17). He is only rejecting roles, neither creating nor discovering the essential self that even at the start he takes as his goal: "The truth was I was not a cynic by nature; only by revolt. I had got away from what I hated, but I hadn't found where I loved, and so I pretended that there was nowhere to love" (17). If centering on an essential self presumes discovering what he loves, Nicholas' quest is hopeless from the start. For reasons that Freud's essay explains, a man like him must always run from what he loves.

From Freud's point of view, abandoning girlfriends is the way Nicholas protects himself against the tenderness that confuses him as his affairs grow beyond desire. Undeserved desertion is his method of degrading or "*lowering* the sexual object in [his] own estimation." Again, he is his own worst enemy. In Freud's scheme of things, degrading the sexual object should renew the "free play" of the male's sensual feeling and restore "considerable sexual capacity and a high degree of pleasure."[5] But Nicholas' pattern of abandonment works at cross-purposes with this goal: having deserted his lover, he is in no position to enjoy this restoration of desire until he can transfer it to a new object.

The nature of Nicholas' problem thus considered is clear and classic. In our literature it is as old as Odysseus' attractions to the opposing figures of Kalypso and Penelope, as modern as Paul Morel's confused feelings about soulful Miriam Leivers and forthright Clara Dawes or Charles Smithson's problems sorting out his relationships with proper Ernestina Freeman and "fallen" Sarah Woodruff in Fowles's *The French Lieutenant's Woman,* published in 1969. What is not as clear is the cause of Nicholas' problem with women. Here both Freud and Jung offer possible explanations, as does Kohut, whose solution has a slightly stronger ring of probability in Nicholas' case than do the earlier models.

Simply put, Freud's analysis of what causes the split between desire and love goes back to the fact that the mother is not only the first

5. *Ibid.,* 208.

object that the male child loves in a tender way but also the first that he desires in an erotic fashion. The confluence of the two currents is normal and fully acceptable, until the age of puberty, when the "currents of libido" grow "far stronger" and run into the "obstacle of the incest-barrier that has in the meanwhile been erected." Thereafter, the male child, in effect, has two mothers or mother images: (1) the mother of whom he is conscious and whom he overestimates as the object of exceedingly tender feelings, and (2) the mother of whom he now must remain unconscious because she is the object of his greatly intensified sensual passion. No longer able to direct his libido toward the real mother, the totally impotent male would have it absorbed in the "creation of phantasy." Less severely disturbed, the psychically impotent male would attempt to dissociate the sensual completely from the tender feelings and direct the former toward a "less exalted" or "ethically inferior" woman, one as different as possible from the "well-brought-up," that is, more motherlike, woman he will find to marry.[6]

The problem with Freud's analysis, as he admits, is that his approach "makes it seem puzzling that [any male] can escape the affliction"; given his analysis, "one would be justified in expecting that psychical impotence was universally prevalent in civilized countries and not a disease of particular individuals." The only way for one "to be really free and happy in love" would be for the male to "overcome his deference for women and come to terms with the idea of incest with mother or sister." Rather than urge this change of heart on Western men, Freud makes this concession: "We shall not be able to deny that the behaviour in love of the men of present-day civilization bears in general the character of the psychically impotent type. In only very few people of culture are the two strains of tenderness and sensuality duly fused into one."[7]

In contrast to Freud's resignation, Conchis in *The Magus* has constructed an elaborate psychodrama to deliver Nicholas from his problem. Conchis and the directors of the godgame would probably not waste their time and resources on Nicholas if his approach to women was not a widespread problem and an important one. Still, their efforts would make no sense if the cause of the problem were as irremediable as what Freud describes. This improbability, along with the enigmatic

6. *Ibid.*, 204–207, 210–11.

7. *Ibid.*, 209–11.

but effective methods Conchis employs, indicates that Conchis has a different cause in mind for Nicholas' emotional impotence—a cause we may describe more completely with Jung's model of the psyche. Here we must reconstruct Nicholas' past by inferring causes from his present actions.

In contrast to the little-noted debt to Freud, Fowles's debt to Jung in *The Magus* has been acknowledged by Fowles in his foreword to the revised version (6) and often noted by critics, beginning with early reviewers.[8] From Jung's perspective and from Fowles's, a great deal more is at stake in the novel than whether young Nicholas Urfe will ever be able to maintain an alliance with a woman. Fowles here has taken on the whole problem of relationship, whether between men and women, men and objects in the world, or men and history. In one of the most provocative colloquies between Nicholas and Conchis, the older man, speaking with less dramatic irony than in other scenes, explains what he considers the distinction between the sexes: "Men see objects, women see the relationship between objects. Whether the objects need each other, love each other, match each other. . . . I will tell you what war is. War is a psychosis caused by an inability to see relationships. Our relationship with our fellow men. Our relationship with our economic and historical situation. And above all our relationship to nothingness. To death" (413). In effect, the older man is telling the younger that as a male he is color-blind to relationships. By implication, Conchis lumps Nicholas with men like Alphonse de Deukans, who is a collector of objects (176–79), and with the Nazi colonel Dietrich Wimmel, who functions as an avenging angel of the SS because his razorlike eyes look at people and see only objects (418–22).

8. Christopher E. Mulvey, in Review of *The Magus,* by John Fowles, in *Commonweal,* April 1, 1966, pp. 60–61, noted that the "'splendid pyrotechnics' of this 'Jungian Disneyland' are marred by the novel's overt moralizing." Since Mulvey's review, at least two dissertations have appeared that consider Fowles from a Jungian perspective, one by Bonnie R. Kates (University of Massachusetts, 1978) and another by Carol M. Barnum (Georgia State University, 1978); Barnum's discoveries will no doubt be included in her forthcoming book, *The Fiction of John Fowles: A Myth for Our Time,* which unfortunately was not available when the present study was written. Robert Huffaker's *John Fowles* (Boston, 1980), 58–65, includes an insightful but general discussion of Jungian aspects of *The Magus*. Barry N. Olshen, in "John Fowles's *The Magus:* An Allegory of Self-Realization," *Journal of Popular Culture,* IX (Spring, 1976), 920–21, comes closer to what I argue but also remains very general.

Through Wimmel, if not through de Deukans as well, *The Magus* as cultural history implies that the excessively masculine manner of seeing only objects reached what has to be its lowest moral point in the historical disasters of the first half of our century. In that period, the habit of separating the mind from the body and from the extended world, in imitation of Descartes—a separation that also made possible many of the scientific and technological splendors of modern Western culture—bottomed out in the hellish experiment with humans and history conducted by Wimmel's Fuhrer.[9]

Because Conchis and his associate Lily de Seitas apparently believe that this masculine way of viewing the world must reverse itself in a radical fashion, they have selected individuals like Nicholas for their improvised psychodramas. In doing so, they implicitly agree with Jung that such individuals determine historical events. In words that foreshadow the daring experiment at Conchis' villa at Bourani, Jung writes: "The great events of world history are, at bottom, profoundly unimportant. In the last analysis, the essential thing is the life of the individual. This alone makes history, here alone do the great transformations first take place, and the whole future, the whole history of the world, ultimately spring as a gigantic summation from these hidden sources in individuals."[10] Jung's notion that history has causes in the psyche of the individual outweighing the material and political factors that we emphasize when we see only objects gives the various masques at Bourani their deepest cultural meaning. If Jung is correct about individuals and history, such changes in men and women as Conchis seeks may be the only way to avoid replicating the disasters of our century. A transformation of this sort, even in a man as insignificant as Nicholas, provides the implicit justification for the excesses, financial, psychological, and ethical, of what Mrs. de Seitas calls the godgame (625).

Drawing upon his earlier association with Jung (224, 234, 337), Conchis has devised a masquelike game that will enable Nicholas, willy-nilly, to develop beyond the male inability to appreciate relationships. First and last, the godgame builds upon relationships in a specifically Jungian fashion. Rather than automatically copy Descartes'

9. Morris Berman, *The Reenchantment of the World* (New York, 1984), 20–22.

10. C. G. Jung, "The Meaning of Psychology for Modern Man," in *Civilization in Transition* (New York, 1964), 148–49.

methodological separation of the thinking subject (the scientist, etc.) from the observed object (the focus of the experiment), Jung restores the older pattern of participatory observation, a step rendered unavoidable, even in the material sciences, by the quantum mechanics of our century.[11] In so doing, Jung uses the complex nature of relationship itself as the basis of his science of culture and the individual psyche. In this way, in accord with Conchis' comment, he restores to modern science the best part of feminine knowledge and in effect, like Conchis, champions the end of positivism. If men, and Cartesian scientists, see only objects upon which they may act expediently, women, because they learn to wait—and the beginning and end of the novel stress waiting—come to know the relationships that creep out from around objects, like living things in a forest, and that though invisible fill the space between the observed and the observer.[12] In his exploration of relationship Jung recognizes that we see things less as they are in themselves than as we the observers are. Rather than despair of this epistemological complication, he makes it the key to psychological understanding: that we "transfer" or project our own unconscious needs and conflicts onto objects, whether a woman, a landscape, a man, or an analyst, is the very philosopher's stone of modern psychology. Properly understood, it is the element that transmutes the dross material of psychological confusion into the uncommon gold of self-knowledge.[13]

Especially powerful and revealing for the Jungians, and central to Nicholas' transformation, are sexual projections in which previously unrecognized emotions, impulses, aspirations, essentially the missing parts of oneself, well up inside. For the attraction of the opposite sex activates the strongest pull of the unconscious on the conscious self; such attraction stretches "consciousness to make space for all that arrives from the unconscious"; it galvanizes "the deepest issues of individuation—that process of differentiating out of unconsciousness one's individual personality in relation to other persons." The feminine part of the unconscious self that a man projects on a woman and needs to reclaim as an element of himself Jung calls the "anima," the part a

11. Berman, *Reenchantment of the World,* 65–66, 141–43.

12. Robert A. Johnson, *She: Understanding Feminine Psychology* (New York, 1977), 41.

13. Jung, *Memories, Dreams, Reflections,* 210 n. 11.

woman projects upon a man, the "animus." In a man, the feminine element, as Conchis contends, is the key to relationships, for the anima is the "projection-making factor" that colors all relationships.[14]

For Jungians, the unconscious content that relationships with the opposite sex bring to consciousness is the material out of which the ego can be enlarged, strengthened, or built. But for growth to occur, the relationship itself, not the object of the sexual desire, must become the focus of the experience. From the Jungian perspective, "all unconscious contents" are "first experienced in *projection,*" which means that "an unconscious quality of one's own is first recognized and reacted to when it is discovered in an outer object." Under ideal circumstances, this transformation of an anima projection into part of the ego would occur in three stages: (1) a symbiotic stage in which the lover takes the beloved as the object of his desires; (2) an analytic stage in which the lover interprets the beloved as a real and separate person upon whom he or she has projected his or her emotions, impulses, aspirations, or other unfinished issues with the opposite sex; and (3) a synthetic stage in which the lover reclaims the parts of the self he or she discovered personified in the beloved.[15] In contrast, the traditional Cartesian split of subject and object, because it seeks to avoid the symbiotic stage, can never benefit from the synthetic state, which is one of personal growth.

Because relationships, for Jungians, are thus the chief, if not the only, means by which the individual develops psychologically, the psychodrama that Conchis and Lily de Seitas and her daughters devise for Nicholas must confront him with a carefully selected series of relationships with both male and female figures. Postponing consideration of the male figures, we note that the psychodrama directed by Conchis expands the types of female images that a man must come to terms with well beyond the acceptable image of the idealized mother and the unacceptable representation of the sensual mother with which Freud's theory of erotic degradation works. In the broader model of Jung, the

14. Ann Bedford Ulanov, "Transference/Countertransference: A Jungian Perspective," in *Jungian Analysis,* ed. Murray Stein (Boulder, 1984), 74–75; C. G. Jung, *Psyche and Symbol: A Selection from the Writings of C. G. Jung,* ed. Violet S. de Laszlo (Garden City, N.Y., 1958), 9, 11.

15. Ulanov, "Transference/Countertransference," 74; Edward F. Edinger, "An Outline of Analytical Psychology," *Quadrant,* I (1968) [Rpr., p. 4].

son may come to realize "that in the realm of his psyche there exists an image of the mother," as with Freud; "not only of the mother" is there an image, however, "but also of the daughter, the sister, the beloved, the heavenly goddess, and the earth spirit." In the male psyche, woman "wears the features of Aphrodite, Helen (Selene), Persephone, and Hecate" and thus reflects the male lack and need for the attributes associated with each of the goddesses. In the more abstract language of Marie-Louise von Franz, the image of woman within a man's psyche expresses itself in four primary stages: the purely instinctual and biological drives; romantic and aesthetic beauty; spiritual love; and wisdom. These four stages may be symbolized, respectively, by Eve, Faust's Helen, the Virgin Mary, and Athena or Wisdom. Each of the stages may manifest itself in two modes, negative (witches, for example) or positive (the Virgin), and the value of each depends on its power over the male or on his perception of its influence.[16]

In other words, even if we accept Freud's concept of the mother's image before and after the incest barrier, Nicholas can potentially respond to more forms of the feminine than those experienced in his own life. His unconscious, according to the Jungian model, is greater than the sum of his repressions; it contains the full range of possible responses he could make as a male of the species. This enlarged repertoire of needs and responses to the feminine derives, in the Jungian system, from the fact that in addition to personal memories of the foremost woman in his own life, Nicholas carries the various archetypes of the feminine that Jung collectively calls the anima—the archetypes being the apparently inborn, universal instincts and patterns of behavior that all men and women share and that present themselves to consciousness in the familiar and recurring figures of myth, religion, legend, fairy tale, dream, and so forth.[17] As a man, Nicholas thus has a much larger range of responses to women than he as an individual has ever known, and it is with this wider range that Conchis works in the long middle section of the novel, where sometimes deliberately, often improvisationally, the character called Lily or Julie presents Nicholas with all the images (masks or representations) of woman his psyche contains hidden away in the deep structures that Jungians call the col-

16. Jung, *Psyche and Symbol*, 11, 20; C. G. Jung *et al.*, *Man and His Symbols* (Garden City, N.Y., 1964), 177–88.

17. Murray Stein, ed., *Jungian Analysis* (Boulder, 1984), 399–400.

lective, as opposed to the personal, unconscious. The intensity of Nicholas' response to each mask and the effectiveness of Conchis' method suggest that in developing the multiple dimensions of Nicholas' anima Conchis is clearly on the right track. Pragmatically speaking, the godgame seems to support the probable truth of Jung's model.

From the start, Conchis appears to know that Nicholas has the habit of leaping into bed with women he will never love, for the psychodrama deliberately reverses the younger man's too-familiar pattern. At the simplest level, Conchis employs Freud's clear split between sensual and ideal images of woman. Even before meeting Conchis, Nicholas has used his idealized image of Greece as a defense against the increasingly tender feelings he and Alison are beginning to share: "What Alison was not to know—since I hardly realized it myself—was that I had been deceiving her with another woman during the latter part of September. The woman was Greece" (39). At this point, Greece is a sufficiently abstract "woman" to protect him from the confusion of desire and love into which Alison draws him. On the island, as Nicholas approaches Conchis' domain, the initial clues the magus plants for him further anesthetize him sensually by calling up projections that steer him away from the erotic: he begins by thinking that Conchis is "simply an old queer" (85), then infers he may be a transvestite (90). Although these projections may hint of some confusion in Nicholas' image of his own sexuality, to the extent that the feminine usually dominates his phantasy life he is himself clearly not homosexual; the early stimuli from Conchis therefore serve chiefly to block his habitual sexual response. Nicholas is reacting to clues from Conchis when he speculates that, among other things, Lily, the still unseen mysterious woman, "might be a mistress, but she might equally well be a daughter, a wife, a sister—perhaps someone weak-minded, perhaps someone elderly" (89). The sexual phantasy comes first but then expands to take in other forms of the feminine before settling on the weak-minded or elderly projection. The latter two guesses imply that part of Nicholas' own anima is crippled and that he will very likely be attracted to a woman he can help.

After Nicholas meets Lily, most of the early parts she enacts in the psychodrama stimulate his crippled anima, appealing to his need to aid her more than to his desire to seduce her. In this first half, whatever role she plays, whether she is a young woman trapped by Conchis in a charade from another time (155–56), the more distant of twin actresses

(201–202), a protected schizophrenic named Julie Holmes, certified incurable, vulnerable but dangerous (*Mg,* 216–20), a victim of Conchis' hypnosis (240, 280–81), an actress held prisoner by Conchis (317), or a young woman left frigid by rape at age thirteen (*Mg,* 327), she calls upon Nicholas' crippled anima, his desire to come to the aid of a woman who needs his help. At the same time, however, she is for Nicholas the archetype she (in the original version) announces herself to be: sister of Apollo, Artemis, the virgin goddess desired by men but forbidden (*Mg,* 177). For the first half of both versions, and for much longer in the original than in the revision, she remains an Artemis figure (in contrast to her Aphrodite-like twin) and so continues to stimulate a more idealized image than Nicholas has ever had to accept in women of his own generation. He quickly comes to value her inaccessible mysteries over the available sexuality of Alison and does so even when his old lover continues to take an interest in him though he has abandoned her for the beauty and pain of Greece (158–59).

It is this less sexual side of Nicholas that Conchis stimulates by recounting the story of his own Lily Montgomery: "Lily was a very pretty girl. But it was her soul that was *sans pareil*" (115). Conchis underscores this point in interpreting his World War I love affair with the prototype of Nicholas' Lily. Describing the restrained sexuality of his own, albeit invented, youth in contrast to the sexual liberties Nicholas takes with Alison and the girls of the 1950s, Conchis defends his own generation: "Perhaps you smile. That we only lay on the ground and kissed. . . . But remember that you have paid a price: that of a world rich in mystery and delicate emotion. It is not only species of animal that die out, but whole species of feeling" (149). In all these actions, the older man is cutting Nicholas off from his habitual sensual relationships in order to bring forth his more delicate emotions, the whole species of feeling he has never experienced with a girl his age. In addition, Nicholas' syphilis panic (symptoms that we later discover were purposefully misdiagnosed by one of Conchis' cronies) serves the same purpose; Nicholas admits, "The crime of syphilis had made me ban sex from my mind for weeks" (159). Under Conchis' management, he is learning to focus on specific qualities he projects on Lily's face, a mirror he finds intelligent and charming, one bespeaking breeding, fastidiousness, delicacy (158)—a face that he uses to defend himself against the temptations in an "unfastidious and not very delicate letter" from Alison inviting him to a reunion in Athens that he imagines as "dirty week-end pleasures . . . in some Athens hotel bedroom" (159).

In the original version of the novel, Lily's role in stimulating Nicholas' delicate emotions persists much longer than in the revised version. In the earlier version, even the hotel scene of Chapter 59 does not permit the two to consummate their protracted courtship. "Do you want me?" the nude Julie asks, holding Nicholas to the bed. "I'm dying for you," Nicholas says. He recounts her strange behavior: "Then very quickly she slipped off the bed; ran to the door. I sat up. 'Julie?' [I said.] She spoke. The strangest voice; as hard as glass. 'There is no Julie' " (*Mg*, 437). Here with three-fourths of the novel behind us, Lily is still "the uncatchable, the virgin temptress" (*Mg*, 436).

The revised version cuts short Lily's role as Artemis for a very specific purpose. It is not Conchis' intent to separate tenderness and desire in Nicholas but to elicit tenderness, then close the gap by making it impossible for him to see women through the dichotomy represented by Aphrodite and Artemis. Although Nicholas' protracted pursuit of Lily in the original version generates mystery, delicate emotions, and desire in the main character (as well as in the reader), it does so artificially, perhaps to the point of prurience or of sexual frustration for the pleasure of the frustration itself. In the revised version, as Fowles underscores in the foreword, "the erotic element is stronger in two scenes" (7) and is fully expressed much earlier in Nicholas' relationship with Lily. For example, by Chapter 46, Lily says, "I am not a virgin, Nicholas" (345). A chapter later, in the little whitewashed chapel, she permits him to caress her breasts without censure (351); and then two short chapters later, in an almost-nude night swim, Lily actually makes love to him with "the gentle rhythm of [her] underwater hand" (369).

Shortly after Lily brings the sensual and tender sides of Nicholas together in this first fully erotic scene, Nicholas receives a clipping from a London newspaper that announces Alison's suicide (396–97). Although his first reaction is to recall the death of his parents in a Karachi air crash (396), the suicide slowly works through his self-pity and other denials to stimulate a remarkable shift of the larger part of his tenderness, his crippled anima perhaps, away from Lily and onto Alison: he recognizes that in his male selfishness he has "imposed the role [he] needed from Alison on her real self" (400), by which he seems to mean that he has crushed the vulnerable, innocent side of her beneath the needs he felt in his "own loins" (400). Now, Alison is not only his wounded Eurydice; she is also the victim of the inhuman Hades in himself. And he has no reason to believe he will ever be Orpheus, or Urfe, enough to bring her back.

This splitting off of his tenderness from Lily and its transfer onto Alison, all of which we later learn was orchestrated by Conchis, constitute a significant shift in the dynamics of Nicholas' inner world. That Conchis originally planned to do more with the absolute split between his subject's erotic and loving sides seems clear from the presence of Lily's identical twin, Rose/June. June, who, according to her sister, has "always been less of a prude" about sex and even "modelled in the nude once" before "it got out" (215), would clearly have been used to stimulate, control, or direct Nicholas' sensual projections according to the requirements of the godgame, partly under the guise of making *Three Hearts,* the film Julie claims Conchis hired the sisters to act in (333, 337). But when Conchis discovers the existence of Alison, or at least the possibility that she will come to Greece, he, if we read between the lines correctly, abandons his original plans for June (who thereafter serves chiefly as a tool of the plot) and abruptly disappears, under the cover of business in Nauplia, a port town very near the island (200), to make new arrangements.

From the moment Alison comes to Conchis' attention until her "suicide," she replaces June as the major carrier of Nicholas' erotic projections (263–69). Faced with choosing between bringing Alison to the island, more tantalization by Lily, or meeting Alison in Athens, Nicholas makes certain that Alison, in all cases, comes out last: "A physical confrontation, even the proximity that Alison's coming to the island might represent, was unthinkable. Whatever happened, if I met her, it must be in Athens. . . . After all I would have Alison to fall back on. I won either way" (203). When they meet, Nicholas repeatedly reminds himself of how poorly Alison measures up to her inaccessible rival: "Alison might launch ten ships in me; but Julie launched a thousand" (246). Or again: "There was something about Alison's manner and appearance; if a man was with her, he went to bed with her. And as I talked, I wondered how we were going to survive the next three days" (248). After Alison shows him how (263) and he again grows confused as his more loving feelings reemerge (264), he decides that quite simply he does love Alison yet wants "to keep—or to find—

Julie" as well: "It wasn't that I wanted one more than the other, I wanted both. I had to have both" (269). This doubling up is not an arrangement Alison can accept (276) or the result Conchis has in mind for Nicholas. But Alison's arranged suicide, coming just after the night swim with Julie, has the desired effect: it increases Alison's nonerotic value in Nicholas' eyes by playing on his crippled anima, the deep feelings of tenderness he can now lavish on the permanently absent Alison. In memory of her, he reads Christopher Marlowe's gentle poem beginning, "Come live with me, and be my love" (400).

After the suicide, with Alison even more inaccessible than the once-virginal Lily, Conchis continues to redirect his subject's projections so that Lily/Julie changes, too; she becomes increasingly the target of his desire and eventually of his deepest hatred. For a moment, as he and Julie make love in the sisters' village house, Nicholas integrates the once-polarized extremes of tenderness and desire (486). This union of opposite emotions is, in a sense, chiefly in his mind, though, for as the girl he thinks he loves tells him, there is no Julie (488). In the trial and disintoxication scenes that follow, Lily quickly picks up Nicholas' projections of negative anima to become a "consummately immoral" actress-prostitute (492), a winged vampire (500), a pregnant but beautiful fish-woman-bird (501), an English witch (504), a clinically unempathic psychologist (512–13), and even an actress in a blue movie (522).

The psychodrama again elicits these projections from Nicholas by parading literal masks before him and by assigning Lily roles to play. She is absolutely correct when she says that there is no Julie; nor, for Nicholas, is there any Lily. There are only the figments of his imagination projected on all the masks Lily/Julie has worn from the first moment he encountered her. Or as Lily de Seitas later says in defense of her girls, "My daughters were nothing but a personification of your own selfishness" (601). They have mirrored him "lie upon lie" because that is their "way of telling the truth" (626) about young men who, unable to see the truth in themselves, can only discover it projected on external objects. In short, they have dramatized the essence of relationships, the very projections that fill the gaps between objects and so connect people one to another. It is appropriate that Lily de Seitas be the player of the godgame to explain this truth to Nicholas, for the ability to see relationships, according to what Conchis asserted earlier, is more often part of feminine genius than masculine.

Because he has become aware of the way he distorts alliances with women, when Alison finally returns, Nicholas, according to Jungian criteria, is readier for her than he has ever been. He has integrated the various sides of his own anima mirrored by Lily well enough to see the Lily-like aspects of Alison: "She was mysterious, almost a new woman. . . . As if what had once been free in her, as accessible as a pot of salt on the table, was now held in a phial, sacrosanct" (650). Better still, he has already decided she is superior to a mystery, better than a forbidden ideal; for she is more constant than Lily (577), freer from changes that bring madness (566), more honest, untreacherous, and real (492–93). He is able now both to love and to desire her.

The effectiveness of the godgame here argues for the value of Jungian theory as Conchis has applied it. He has provided stimuli and screens (primarily Lily but also Alison) that force Nicholas to project a full range of anima figures he needs to experience and then accept, if he is to free himself from projections that have generally doomed his relationships. Conchis' use of such figures as Artemis, Aphrodite, Miranda, Ariadne, vampires, witches, and Astarte (the oriental goddess before the Greeks divided her powers in order to conquer them) to guide Nicholas' growth indicates that Conchis subscribes to the Jungian concept that unclaimed archetypes of the feminine, called the anima, cause such projections. We can go on to argue that Nicholas eventually comes to terms with the crippled part of his anima by learning to value what he sees mirrored in Kemp, his London landlady, and JoJo, his short-term companion; in respecting them despite their dumpiness, he is able to love unseemly parts of himself. That the masque of archetypes works as well as it does suggests that the initial problem lay in Nicholas' ignorance of the various energies his undeveloped anima contained.

If we step outside the guidelines Fowles provides in the foreword to the revised version, however, and view the book using a psychological model created since the novel was first written, that of Kohut, we may discover less controversial causes for Nicholas' behavior than ignored archetypes of the feminine. Kohut's approach also provides an alternative explanation of the reasons the masque works and suggests ways it could have worked better, that is, well enough not to leave readers angry about Conchis' manipulation of Nicholas.

From Kohut's perspective, in contrast to Jung's or even Freud's, Nicholas' memories of his parents take on more significance in explaining the source of his behavior both with Conchis and with the various women. For Kohut places great importance on the success of maternal figures in mirroring a child well enough to give it a solid sense of its own worthiness and on the success of paternal figures in providing a model the child can idealize in an appropriate fashion. From the first of the primary figures, the child receives its basic ambitions, and from the second, its ideals. A child, in the summarizing language of Ernest S. Wolf, "needs to be assured [by a mirroring parent] of its value, importance, and even its illusionary grandiosity"; the child also "needs the availability of a calm, strong, wise, beautiful, and idealizable selfobject into which he [or she] can feel merged" and eventually thereby learn to imitate. Kohut calls these essential parenting figures "selfobjects" because at this stage in life a child experiences them as parts of itself as much as it does as objects in its environment. Only if the early selfobjects fulfill these two roles will the child develop a cohesive self that Kohut calls the core or "nuclear self."[18] In defining this nuclear self, Kohut describes its structure and purpose: "[It] is the basis for our sense of being an independent center of initiative and perception, integrated with our most central ambitions and ideals and with our experience that our body and mind form a unit in space and a continuum in time. This cohesive and enduring psychic configuration, in connection with a correlated set of talents and skills that it attracts to itself or that develops in response to the demands of the ambitions and ideals of the nuclear self, forms the central sector of the personality" (*RS,* 177–78). Lacking a cohesive self, a man or a woman will seek to hide this deficiency and to deny the ensuing low self-esteem by unconsciously constructing an archaic "grandiose self" that restores some of the harmony, elation, and omnipotence felt in the earliest periods of life when the child was still fused physically or emotionally with its mother.[19] Because this inflated self is a false self, a merely defensive structure, it is exceedingly vulnerable and when im-

18. Ernest S. Wolf, "Psychoanalytic Psychology of the Self and Literature," *New Literary History,* XII (1980), 43–44; *RS,* 31–32.

19. *Cf.* Bela Grunberger, *Narcissism: Psychoanalytic Essays,* trans. Joyce S. Diamanti (New York, 1979), 20. Fowles has sanctioned the quest for this reunion with "the vanished young mother of infancy," "that eternal other woman," for the search is essential to his own creative impulse and, he suggests, to the creativity of many other novelists. See John Fowles, "Hardy and the Hag," in *Thomas Hardy After Fifty Years,* ed. Lance St. John Butler (Totowa, N.J., 1977), 33, 35, 40. Fowles's *Mantissa,* published in 1982, records the difficulties of the search for this muse.

periled to the point of fragmentation responds with a variety of behaviors (including rage, sadism, and compulsive sexual activity) that seek to ward off the resulting anxiety with a poorly revitalized, infantile grandiosity.

When we turn from Kohut's perspective to what Nicholas tells us, we cannot help but notice missing elements in his relationships with both parents: "I had long before made the discovery that I lacked the parents and ancestors I needed" (15). Although this early sentence refers specifically to the social and intellectual inferiority he feels when he goes to Oxford, where he "began to discover [he] was not the person [he] wanted to be" (15), it also contains a significant clue to his psychological emptiness. He reports of his mother: "[She] was the very model of a would-be major-general's wife. That is, she never argued with [her husband] and always behaved as if he were listening in the next room, even when he was thousands of miles away" (15). The implication is that she was cold and distant to the boy rather than warm and assuring. His father, as he remembers him, was generally absent, "and in his long absences I used to build up a more or less immaculate conception of him which he generally—a bad but appropriate pun—shattered within the first forty-eight hours of his leave" (15).

The comments are suggestive. Nicholas' dissatisfaction with his father as an ideal underlies the rankling hurt in the pun by which he seeks to make light of his father's never rising above the rank of brigadier. We can accept at face value Nicholas' report (it is all we have to go on) that his mother was a model military wife. Or we can infer from the reference to his father's listening from the next room thousands of miles away a guilt shared by mother and son because she reacted, as wives of absent husbands traditionally have, by spoiling her son with the affection she could not lavish on the boy's father.[20] Either way, Nicholas did not receive the healthy mirroring or the idealizable model he needed, in Kohut's view, to develop a cohesive nuclear self. The best evidence to support this conclusion arises from his efforts at

20. Philip E. Slater, *The Glory of Hera: Greek Mythology and the Greek Family* (Boston, 1968), 30–31, 426–27. This pattern was first brought to my attention by Cheryle Lamberth Shaffer, "Maternal Relationships in the Early Novels of John Fowles" (M.A. thesis, University of North Carolina, 1989).

Oxford to compensate with various aesthetic, cynical, and superficially existential poses (16–17), all false and overly grand.

Similarly, using Kohut's model, we would argue that Nicholas' repeated failures to sustain intimacy with girls betray the hollowness of his essential self, an emptiness he attempts to cover with the inflation and superficial vitality of frequent conquests. He cannot love because, at the core, he does not feel worthy of love. In Kohut's language, "sexual activity . . . [including] the need for the incessant, self-reassuring performance of sexual exploits by certain Don Juan types, has the aim of counteracting a sense of self depletion or of forestalling the danger of self fragmentation" (*AS*, 119 n. 5).

Viewed from Kohut's model, Conchis inadvertently does very nearly the right things for Nicholas but for the wrong reason. What Nicholas needs, from this perspective, is not more archetypes of the feminine but better selfobjects. And selfobjects are what Conchis provides, even though he generally disguises them as masks of mythical females. Or we may want to call them "transitional objects," for they function much as D. W. Winnicott's transitional objects do. Moreover, they are offered to Nicholas at Bourani, a realm of illusion that parallels the transitional space in which a child gains the confidence necessary for imaginative living and creativity. Conchis' disintoxication process may owe something to Winnicott's "gradual disillusionment process," by which one is weaned from dependence upon illusions about the mother's omnipresence and the potency of transitional objects.[21] Conchis' hope for Nicholas is that by experiencing empathic selfobjects that mirror new sides of his personality or that provide models to idealize, he will gradually develop a more cohesive nuclear self. This is what happens, even though the language used to describe the process is the language of Jung and myth, not that of Kohut.

Although Lily, Rose, and their mother Mrs. de Seitas at times seem to lack sympathy for Nicholas, they empathize enough to mirror and

21. See D. W. Winnicott, "Transitional Objects and Transitional Phenomena," in *Playing and Reality* (London, 1971), 12–13. Winnicott's concepts, his nationality, and the original date of his key article (1953) might argue for a direct influence on the creation of Bourani. Fowles, however, reports, "Of Winnicott [I know] a very little; rather as one knows of ghosts!" He adds, in reference to his novel in progress: "I used once only to need ghosts . . . to body out the fictional 'reality'" (John Fowles to Julius Rowan Raper, January 8, 1989). Much of Winnicott's theory Kohut has expanded on.

confirm him in ways that expand his usual range of responses to women. In the anima phases described in the Jungian section above, the women of the godgame help him experience the tenderer dimensions of his personality that all his other affairs have failed to develop. They may not assist him in the effective manner Kohut recommends for psychotherapy, but by the end, Nicholas has sufficiently changed to find mysteries in Alison where formerly he saw only her bruised innocence.

At the same time, Conchis is working in a parallel fashion to develop Nicholas' nuclear self, to make it more cohesive and solid, by providing important models of maleness for him to imitate and reject. Although the godgame includes almost as many masks of the masculine as of the feminine, Conchis develops three basic roles; he is Prospero (the good father), Minos, or the Minotaur (the monster), and Hades (the god or father who absconds). As Prospero (83), the millionaire collector of Modigliani's works (92–93) and lovely young women (119), Conchis plays the role of a man Zeus-like (80), Picasso-like, saurian, the "quintessential Mediterranean man" (81), which Nicholas not only envies (82) but longs to imitate—a longing that his assuming the role of Ferdinand, obedient suitor of Prospero's daughter Miranda (83), betrays. As an idealizable father, Conchis speaks to Nicholas of his own (perhaps invented) cowardness during World War I, a confession that potentially frees Nicholas from the guilt he feels for rejecting his own military father (126–27).

When Conchis changes his role as good father, he signals it blatantly by sneaking up on Nicholas and Julie armed with a four-foot axe, which he holds poised "exactly as if he were in two minds about raising and sinking it in [Nicholas'] skull" (291). Conchis has earlier come between the young lovers effectively enough to pick up Nicholas' unresolved feelings about his own father: "A hostility was at last proclaimed; a clash of wills. . . . We both knew we smiled to hide a fundamental truth: that we could not trust each other one inch" (228). To Conchis' acting as the barrier between him and Lily/Julie, Nicholas reacts by taking on the grandiose role of Theseus as detective and musing that "somewhere in the darkness Ariadne waited; and perhaps the Minotaur" (313). Nicholas now regards Conchis as "the old man" who feeds him lies, "some animal in a den . . . to be coaxed out a little more . . . trapped and destroyed" (322). Still eliciting Nicholas' Oedipal feelings, Conchis tells his visitor of Henrik Nygard's God, cruel, unjust, inaccessible, and patriarchal (302–309), and of the absolute nadir of European patriarchy, represented by the murderous conduct of Wimmel (418–33). At the same time, he provides two models of positive male assertion, each arising from a seemingly solid psychological center: the Cretan guerilla's affirmation of a primal Greek freedom (*eleutheria*) beyond good and evil (425, 433–34) and Conchis' own difficult decision to act from the same core in himself by refusing to club the two surviving Cretans to death (433–35).

It is Conchis' third major role, the absconding god, however, that finally leads Nicholas to the discovery of his own essential role, that of Orpheus to Alison's Eurydice and to Conchis' invisible Hades. According to Kohut's theory, Nicholas' experiences of Conchis as an empathic and mature idealizable selfobject should lead to the "gradual acquisition" of the coherent self, felt as an inner "firmness, vigor, vitality, and harmoniousness." Such wholeness would increase his capacity to soothe himself without depending on outside help (*HDAC,* 65–66). Such self-soothing would mark a significant change; for not only has Nicholas habitually needed expendable young women in order to feel complete, but he has also been dependent, like Nygard and like Nicholas' mother in his father's absence, on an invisible, ubiquitous third person for whom he has impersonated his life: "Always I had acted as if a third person was watching and listening and giving me marks for good or bad behaviour—a god like a novelist, to whom I turned, like a character with the power to please, the sensitivity to feel slighted, the ability to adapt himself to whatever he believed the novelist-god wanted. This leech-like variation of the superego I had created myself, fostered myself, and because of it I had always been incapable of acting freely" (539). Out of this need for an omniscient observer, Nicholas has always tried to turn his life into a fiction and in the process has held life away from himself (539, *cf.* 347–48). Clearly, this habit is the result of his unfinished business with a father who, because he was always absent, never gave his son the opportunity to experience and work out the full range of emotions sons have about fathers, feelings that run from absolute idealization to Oedipal hatred.

The habitual sensation that he is "not alone," that he is "being looked at" (68), is what fills his mind immediately before he receives his first messages from Conchis (69). His final thought of Conchis is in sharp contrast: "There were no watching eyes. . . . The theatre was empty. It [Cumberland Terrace, the world] was not a theatre" (654).

The magi and mythical monsters are all unmasked; they are merely stone statues. Conchis and the rest of the godgame's pantheon have absconded. Nicholas and Alison are alone, frozen in true hazard, mere fragments of freedom (655–66). Having come to understand the projections and selfobjects that govern relationships, Nicholas has, in effect, ceased to see himself as a mere object acting for others.

From Kohut's perspective, Conchis has done a much better job extinguishing Nicholas' dependence on fathers than his need for women. Admittedly, his "father" has disappeared again, but this time Nicholas has internalized the ability to take care of himself. He no longer needs to invent the leechlike superego, "the terrible faceless Avenging God of the Bourgeois British," their "ubiquitous person of speech," their "One" (560). This final absconding of the One-who-watches-and-does-this-or-does-not-do-that, he decides, with some resentment, is the "perfect climax of the godgame" (655). In contrast to this closure with fathers, he warns Alison at the end that if "Lily walked down that path behind us and beckoned to me . . . I don't know [what I would do]" (653; ellipsis in the original). That he cannot predict how he would respond to Lily shows that he still is far from free of his female phantasies.

If, from Kohut's perspective, Conchis has succeeded better in freeing Nicholas from his dependence on fathers than in releasing him from his need for the feminine, the reason seems to be that Conchis has frustrated the former need in a gradual fashion, whereas the separation from Lily that Conchis engineered was far too abrupt. Kohut places great importance on appropriate frustration. In a deliberately reifying image of the process he calls "optimal frustration," he suggests that the core or nuclear self, like an atom, is made up of psychological "microstructures," that is, "engrams of memory traces and ideas" (*RS,* 31 n. 5). Such microstructures are internalized whenever a parent or an analyst, or another selfobject, frustrates an individual's needs for mirroring or for an ideal model at the rate necessary for that individual to learn to perform for himself or herself whatever soothing behavior he or she formerly expected from the selfobject: "through the process of transmuting internalization, new psychological structure is built" (*RS,* 32; *HDAC,* 69–70). The classic example is the behavior of a mother who somehow knows exactly how long to increase periods between feedings so that a child who has depended on her attention (as much as her breast) learns to soothe itself with toes, fingers, or toys. Conchis, in effect, starts frustrating Nicholas' need for an idealizable male with the early story of Alphonse de Deukans, the wealthy Frenchman who played the part in Conchis' career that Nicholas obviously dreams Conchis will play in his own: de Deukans left the magus a large part of his fortune (187). But the wealthy French collector, a misogynist whose grotesque denial of the feminine leads to suicide (187), is far less admirable than Conchis and, as a variation of Conchis, provides a cautionary mirror of the collector side of Nicholas. After de Deukans, Conchis' gradual rejection of the roles Nicholas expects from him continues, intermittently, through the other episodes of the novel until he vanishes, setting his would-be dependent free.

Lily, though, first tantalizes Nicholas, then gradually sexualizes their relationship, and finally and abruptly frustrates him with the reversals that start after their intoxicating sexual union (486) and continue through the trial and the accompanying disintoxication scenes. These startling scenes succeed as literature, which is their ultimate purpose, but at the same time reveal the partial failure of the godgame. They do not really offer Nicholas an optimal process of frustration. The reversals in his experiences here are simply too abrupt for him to learn to soothe himself and thereby establish the inner wholeness that would allow him to tolerate Lily's imagined return without either fragmenting or feeling sexual drives he could not resist.

In short, Kohut provides ground a reader can stand on while evaluating the psychodrama in *The Magus* as well as a boundary to place around the seeming omniscience of Conchis and the two Lilies, who have led the unwitting reader through the masques much the way they have Nicholas. To frame the godgame thus in no way reduces the book's effectiveness as a novel. Nor does the use of Kohut's model claim to exhaust the book's meanings, not even the psychological ones. Nor, finally, does the application of this contemporary approach deny the usefulness of the Freudian model in clarifying Nicholas' problem at its simplest level or the appropriateness of the Jungian theory of the anima in describing the maze of mirrors through which the masques run Nicholas. Bringing Kohut into the picture, however, confirms the brilliance of Fowles's intuitions in creating the godgame; it shows the high degree to which Fowles has anticipated a number of the most effective concepts of contemporary psychological theory and practice.

Indeed, Kohut's approach confirms the main point the godgame appears to make: that the inability of separate individuals to deal with one another while drawing on a solid nuclear self (Kohut) or individuated self (Jung) and without unrealistic expectations or irrational rages constitutes the basic problem out of which the pathology of cultural groups emerges.[22] Jung phrases it in this way: "When we look at human history, we see only what happens on the surface. . . . The true historical event lies deeply buried, experienced by all and observed by none. It is the most private and most subjective of psychic experiences. Wars, dynasties, social upheavals, conquests, and religions are but the superficial symptoms of a secret psychic attitude unknown, even to the individual himself, and transmitted by no historian."[23] If the godgame enables a few callous, insecure individuals like Nicholas Urfe to change their psychic attitudes enough to see relationships rather than objects, that may be a start for an entire culture trapped in the myth of objective knowledge. This transformation at least appears to be the secret intent of Conchis, Lily de Seitas, and John Fowles himself.

22. Heinz Kohut, *Self Psychology and the Humanities,* ed. Charles B. Strozier (New York, 1985), 208, 220, 227.

23. Jung, "Meaning of Psychology," 148–49.

IV The Chameleon and the Narcissists: Jerzy Kosinski's *Being There*

The progress Fowles's Nicholas Urfe makes in constructing a solid core self is nowhere visible in Jerzy Kosinski's *Being There,* for it is difficult to imagine a more decentered character than Kosinski's protagonist. His minor characters, however, have their own centers for initiating projects that mark them as narcissists of an amusing, thoroughly human type.

In his first novels, *The Painted Bird* and *Steps,* published in 1965 and 1968, respectively, Kosinski created protagonists who have no names and little or no interiority, who are primarily the things they perceive and experience, and who therefore are suitable witnesses to recount the horrors of modern history. The characters' behavior and Kosinski's comments about them indicate that he was working with an existential model of individual being. It is appropriate then that in his third novel, *Being There,* published in 1971, he should foreground the existential model of "human life" beginning with the title that translates Martin Heidegger's central concept, *Dasein,* itself the working title of the novel.[1] One could scarcely imagine a more compelling literary allusion than the title Kosinski settled on. Yet through Chance, the novel's central character, Kosinski satirizes Dasein in a manner at once gentle and penetrating. Chance is an exaggeration of the Protean, and

1. *Cf.* Norman Lavers, *Jerzy Kosinski* (Boston, 1982), 67–69, 126.

phenomenological, character type that Pynchon calls the soul-transvestite.[2]

What makes the Protean theme in *Being There* especially valuable is that Kosinski skillfully plays Chance off against a contrary group of characters who are narcissists of a sometimes disagreeable, yet altogether human sort. Whereas in Pynchon's *V.* all the characters are overtly phenomenological in conception and Freudian only by implication, in *Being There* both types are presented explicitly, and both are satirized. The tones used in the treatment of the two groups of characters vary so greatly, however, that the reader may overlook the fine conceptual balance of the novel—a balance that provides a warning about contemporary social critics.

Chance is a very gentle man and, according to Kosinski, retarded.[3] Given Chance's traits, readers generous with their sentiments are understandably reluctant to deal harshly with the character, but sentimentalism is not among the shortcomings generally ascribed to Kosinski (if we except changes he made in the ending of the story to prepare it for a film audience). Consequently, when we read *Being There,* we must be prepared to treat Chance as realistically as we treat the other characters. When we do so, we discover that Kosinski, in this seemingly simple parable, has taken on the opposition between psychological and phenomenological models of behavior, a central problem of the late twentieth century.

Both the existential and the narcissist elements in the book were noted by the earliest commentators. Clarence W. Richey, for example, discussed Kosinski's debt to one quality of Dasein, what Heidegger called the "thrownness" (*Gerworfenheit*) of our human reality, our having "been abruptly 'hurled' or 'thrown' into the alien muddle of . . . mysterious Existence" without knowing the purpose or goal of our being here. For Richey, Chance is a "characterless chameleon" who "becomes whomever he sees, easily and indifferently assuming whatever form the prejudices and expectations of his fellows may impose upon him." John M. Gogol, in contrast, calls Chance a modern Narcissus who falls "in love with the image projected on his television screen." To support his case, Gogol has to argue that Kosinski, to some

2. Pynchon, *V.,* 226, 440.
3. Lavers, *Jerzy Kosinski,* 80.

extent, "subverts the original" myth so that the image (on the screen or in the water) "precedes the original" (Chance or Narcissus) and dominates the living original at the same time that it controls it.[4]

Although Richey does not develop the implications of Chance's relationship to Dasein, his claim appears less strained than Gogol's. Yet Gogol, too, is in many ways correct, for the echoes of Narcissus in *Being There* are strong ones. We must first recognize, however, that though Chance is too retarded to be a true narcissist, he nonetheless is the sort of character who finds himself "thrown," in good Heideggerian fashion, into an incomprehensible world. Seeing Chance clearly in this way, as a phenomenologically conceived character with a number of narcissistic traits, we can shift our perspective 180 degrees and notice that the other characters are totally narcissistic in their dealings with him.

When we view Chance from Heidegger's perspective, we quickly note that the emphasis falls on the "there," or *da,* part of Dasein, not the "being," or *sein,* part. In the opening pages of the novel, the narrator gives us this remarkable description of Chance watching television: "By changing the channel he could change himself. . . . He could change as rapidly as he wished by twisting the dial backward and forward. In some cases he could spread out into the screen without stopping, just as on TV people spread out into the screen."[5] This is the aspect of human life that Sartre stresses when discussing Heidegger: "*Dasein* is 'outside of itself, in the world'; it is 'a being of distances.' . . . *Dasein* 'is not' in itself . . . it 'is not' in immediate proximity to itself."[6] With Sartre's description in mind, it is difficult to imagine a character, other than perhaps Herbert Stencil in *V.,* who more completely exists not inside himself but outside in the world.

Like a character in a novel of manners, Chance monitors the outside world continuously for clues to the way he should act: "Chance knew that he should not reveal that he could not read or write. On TV programs people who did not know how to read or write were mocked

4. Clarence W. Richey, "'Being There' and *Dasein:* A Note on the Philosophical Presupposition Underlying the Novels of Jerzy Kosinski," *Notes on Contemporary Literature,* II (September, 1972), 13, 15; John M. Gogol, "Kosinski's Chance: McLuhan Age Narcissus," *Notes on Contemporary Literature,* I (September, 1971), 9.

5. Jerzy Kosinski, *Being There* (New York, 1970), 5; hereinafter cited parenthetically by page number in the text.

6. Sartre, *Being and Nothingness,* 18.

and ridiculed" (23). Consequently, with the Old Man's lawyers, he pretends to read a waiver of claims against the Old Man's estate, then ambiguously says he "can't sign it" (24). With other characters, his conduct is largely imitative and lacking in spontaneity. With EE Rand, for example, "thinking that he ought to show a keen interest in what EE [is] saying, Chance [resorts] to repeating to her parts of her own sentences, a practice he [has] observed on TV" (37). Because other people dominate him as completely as they do Eliza Doolittle at the Ascot Opening Day, his character is as much a product of his environment as was John Locke's man as a tabula rasa. Eliza and Locke's man differ from Chance and other men and women in the late twentieth century, however, because for the contemporary group a single environment, television, has very nearly displaced all other environments. At the Rands' home, for example, "in deciding how to behave, Chance chose the TV program of a young businessman who often dined with his boss and the boss's daughter" (39).

Such passages, of which there are a number, reveal how completely Chance's Dasein, his Being, has been, in Heidegger's terminology, ensnared in the world around him, to what extent he interprets himself "in terms of that world by its reflected light." Over and over, Chance illustrates the potentiality of all Dasein to fall "prey to the things in the world," to become "alienated to its own authentic possibilities, intentions and endeavours."[7] For most individuals, according to Heidegger, this tendency to fall (*Verfallen*) is chiefly a potentiality. With Chance, it dominates his Being.

Chance "falls" into the world so frequently because he lacks several other characteristics Heidegger ascribes to Being. First, when Heidegger describes this sort of fall, he speaks of Being that is "actively concerned with beings" (*zuhanden*) that "belong to the realm of civilisation," of existence that "gets caught up in issues and affairs of the moment." But Chance takes his coloration indiscriminately, and almost mindlessly, from other beings who, unlike him, have projects of their own and from things that are simply "there by nature," or *vorhan-*

7. Martin Heidegger, *Basic Writings from "Being and Time" (1927) to "The Task of Thinking" (1964),* ed. David Farrell Krell (New York, 1977), 65–66; Werner Brock, "An Account of 'Being and Time,'" in *Existence and Being,* by Martin Heidegger (Chicago, 1949), 28.

den.[8] In addition, Heidegger's stress on active concern, issues, and affairs presumes a project or purpose flowing from an initiatory center that Chance lacks. In a sense, everything in Chance's outer world is given rather than chosen. He does not initiate; he only responds, like the plants he once cared for. "No plant can do anything intentionally: it cannot help growing, and its growth has no meaning, since a plant cannot reason or dream" (3). Chance is equally passive.

In one sense, Chance is more passive than a chameleon, for a chameleon changes only its outward appearance to blend with the surroundings. With Chance, the inner world, too, is given rather than chosen. In the passage describing his interaction with EE, the narrator tells us, "Her words seemed to float inside his head; he observed her as if she were on television" (37). When he watches the television, not only does he sink "into the screen," but "the world from outside the garden [enters] Chance" (6). Consequently, in him, the pedagogy of television has produced a character even more the victim of contemporary soul-transvestism than was Herbert Stencil in *V.* Stencil had to "dislocate his personality forcibly" into the point-of-view characters who observe V., the object of his quest; Chance has merely to switch channels in order to float, "like a TV image . . . into the world, buoyed up by a force he did not see and could not name" (6). In Chance, the Cosmic Will of Arthur Schopenhauer has given way to the collective will of the networks.

Although Kosinski clearly intends the novel as a savage attack on the television culture of the late twentieth century, television is not solely responsible for the passivity of Chance.[9] Heidegger's analysis enables us to identify characteristics of Dasein lacking in Chance that would have enabled him to respond to his television-dominated environment with greater powers of choice. For Heidegger, Dasein exhibits, along with its fallenness, the characteristics he calls "existentiality" and "facticity" (*Befindlichkeit* or *Faktizität*). Viewed in relation to either quality, Chance is exceptional.

Existentiality, for example, means that Dasein "is concerned about its own Being," that it exists " 'for the sake of' its own Being." Everything we see of Chance indicates that he is not sufficiently self-

8. Brock, "Account of 'Being and Time,' " 14, 50; Heidegger, *Basic Writings,* 22.

9. David Sohn, "A Nation of Videots," *Media and Methods,* XI (April, 1975), 25.

reflective to "care" (another key concept for Heidegger) very much about Being.[10] In fact, he sees no difference between a man he watches on television and the face he sees in the mirror and so immediately becomes one with the former face and voice (6).

The third fundamental trait of Dasein, facticity, signifies that Dasein normally has a past, a history, before it finds itself in the world. "It is always already in a world . . . in advance of itself." Heidegger says of it: "Dasein always is as and 'what' it already was. Whether explicitly or not, it *is* its past. . . . Its past, as it were, pushes itself along 'behind' it, and . . . it possesses what is past as a property that is still objectively present and at times has an effect on it."[11] Chance lacks a past, in part, because his circumstances have robbed him of legal parents, even though the Old Man may be his biological father (8); have left him without official documentation (16); and have uprooted him from the only home he has ever known (24, 27). In a certain sense, these circumstances would themselves constitute Chance's past.

His rootlessness has a deeper cause, however, than outward circumstances. What the Old Man tells Chance about himself and his mother, that they both were severely brain damaged (8), subsequent events substantiate, and the damage affects Chance's memory. He has some short-term memory, for in the Rands' house he is able to recollect the traditional wisdom of his gardening days with the Old Man (54). But his short-term memory is limited: it is rote memory, in which particulars from his present setting, his conversations with Benjamin Rand and the President, for example, remain unassimilated.

When we examine his long-term memory, we discover that television, among other things, offers an especially appropriate mirror of his mind. A television set has no memory, neither short- nor long-term. The ultimate limit of Chance's memory becomes obvious in the final scene. As he leaves the party at which the boys in the backroom are preparing to nominate him for high political office (president or vice-president of the United States?), he passes "through a blaze of photographers' flash-guns as through a cloud." All this light short-circuits his memory: "The image of all he had seen outside the garden faded. . . . He reflected and saw the withered image of Chauncey Gardiner; it was cut by the stroke of a stick through a stagnant pool of rain. His own

10. Brock, "Account of 'Being and Time,'" 49–51.

11. *Ibid.*, 50; Heidegger, *Basic Writings*, 64.

image was gone as well. . . . Not a thought lifted itself from Chance's brain. Peace filled his chest" (139–40). In this final scene (which differs significantly from the film ending, where Kosinski turns Chance into a Christ figure, or parody thereof, walking miraculously on water), the channels of Chance's Being have changed again, switched this time by external events, the overload of the flash-guns on his damaged nervous system. Because his short-term memory has been erased, the continuity of his long-term memory is totally disrupted.

Apparently Chance's memory lives for a season, and passes through cycles like plants in a garden. As a result, his Dasein has no past to push itself along behind his present Being. His facticity puts no weight on his present Being, for its erasures periodically free him from the anguish or anxiety of true Being. He lives in an eternal present without the past, or future, that would characterize fully human life. In this way, Chance actually resembles Heidegger's Dasein less than Sartre's Being-for-itself, for Sartre speaks of a free human consciousness transcending its intolerable past toward an impossible future object. Chance, however, experiences none of the anxiety or anguish that is the mark of Being for both Heidegger and Sartre.[12] He is pure Dasein without human complexity and so only marginally human, as all the plant comparisons in the novel imply. As a literary character, he is a satirical exaggeration of the personality type implicit in Heidegger's Dasein and Sartre's Being-for-itself: he *is* consciousness of objects in a culture where the television screen has become the object sine qua non.

None of the other characters are so completely adapted to the age of television. If becoming a "videot" (95) is the mark of the fully modern man in the milieu Kosinski describes, then the other characters are simply old-fashioned people and narcissists of an all-too-human sort. Each of the others has a hidden agenda and an interior space in which to hide it. Each has an inner world of needs, fears, drives, ambitions, and dreams, and each fills the blankness of Chance with his or her narcissistic projects. These projects are more than mere facticity, however, more than by-products of a past to be overcome. Their drives and dreams are relatively autonomous energies grounded in an individual past that is part biological, part environmental—a past that works in the present to guarantee the preservation and perhaps realiza-

12. Sartre, *Being and Nothingness*, 29.

tion of their drives and dreams in the future. Such projects in large part exist outside (or beneath) the consciousness of the individuals yet work to create the individuality of their consciousness. Contrary to Sartre's view of consciousness as freedom, such projects do not exist to be transcended by consciousness but are themselves the essence of individual consciousness.

For the world into which Chance has fallen, against which he brushes, through which he at times almost floats, merely *seems* one, in Heidegger's terms, of idle talk, vain curiosity, and ambiguity.[13] In fact, however, the creatures of his new world are pursuing much more specific projects than Heidegger's categories imply.

Chance's conversations with the Rands, the President, Ambassador Skrapinov, and others have the appearance of Heidegger's "idle talk" in that they deal with public and clichéd topics: gardens (39), the changing seasons (54), Wall Street (54), and Russian fables (90). Because these are topics that "anyone can rake up," such social chats hold out the possibility of one "understanding everything without previously [working to make] the thing one's own." In such conversations one generally has no conscious aim to deceive but only wishes to close off exploration of truth by seeming already to understand everything. In this way, everything said becomes hearsay, too obvious to warrant new inquiry or disputation. It is the sense one has at a cocktail party where everyone has read that Sunday's New York *Times* or the latest translation of a work by Jacques Derrida. Real discourse turns groundless and so becomes a barrier to disclosing the true nature of one's human Being. A public "they" thus "prescribes one's state-of-mind, and determines what and how one 'sees.'" An individual engaged in idle talk begins to feel uprooted from understanding and seems to "float unattached."[14] Because such rootless chattering, such inauthenticity, forms so large a part of social conversations, EE, Rand, the President, and Skrapinov feel no need to press Chance on the topics mentioned and so never discover that he knows absolutely nothing about any subject except gardening.

Probably because idle talk is empty, one falls, according to Heideg-

13. Martin Heidegger, *Being and Time,* trans. John Macquarrie and Edward Robinson (New York, 1962), 220–21.

14. *Ibid.,* 213–14.

ger, into pointless curiosity. Chance's curiosity, his openness to the Rands as well as to others he encounters once he leaves the Old Man's garden and his interest in the activities of the television studio (63), appears so positive a trait that it helps keep the reader from assessing his behavior realistically. Because the distinction between what Chance is thinking and what the narrator is telling us becomes blurred, the uncritical reader may mistake Chance for the noble creature of whom Aristotle spoke when he said that "all men by nature desire to know." For Heidegger, however, curiosity is that sort of knowing in which one wishes to see something "not in order to understand what is seen . . . but *just* in order to see." Curiosity "seeks restlessness" and novelty and encounters as distractions: it never dwells anywhere, is everywhere and nowhere, is "constantly uprooting itself."[15] Because rootlessness is the mark of Chance's limited memory, the critical reader recognizes that Chance's seeing is not a way of knowing or understanding what he sees but rather a form of curiosity even less substantial, if possible, than what Heidegger describes.

In much the way Heidegger speaks of, Chance's response to the idle talk around him, along with his curiosity about television, the President, the powerful men and women he meets in his brief progress from the garden of his childhood to political candidacy, generates terrifying but hilarious ambiguities. Where everything seems genuinely understood, taken hold of, "though at bottom it is not," the task of deciding "what is [truly understood] and what is not" soon "becomes impossible." Where everyone discusses subjects by scenting out in advance what for others already goes without saying, idle talk goes on to the topic that is newest, and what is genuinely new or created is kept always out of date. With hearsay and things unsaid dominating conversations, ambiguity thrives.[16] As a result of what Chance leaves unsaid, EE Rand takes him as a confidant and replacement for her dying husband (36–37), Benjamin Rand assumes he is a wise and productive businessman (40), the President believes he is a profound champion of tight-money economics (57), and Ambassador Skrapinov mistakes him for an American businessman willing to deal with the Soviet bloc (99). Each character has turned blanks in Chance's behavior and am-

15. *Ibid.*, 215 n. 2, 216–17.

16. *Ibid.*, 217–18.

biguities in his conversation into forthright statements of what Chance in fact has left unthought as well as unspoken. Such misunderstandings have the appearance of Heideggerian ambiguities.

Closer attention, though, shows that Kosinski's seemingly idle talk is never truly idle, that the curiosity of the characters other than Chance is never truly vain, that Chance's ambiguities are never interpreted in a pointless way. To understand what is happening in his scenes with EE, the President, and the other characters, we need to move from a phenomenological approach to a more completely psychological analysis of what goes on in Chance's encounters.

The pattern presented by the other, "normal" characters reveals that a very simple, totally normal narcissism is at work. EE, Rand, the President, and the rest do not see Chance as he is; they see him as they are. The pattern is so simple that it scarcely bears pointing out, except that it implies a good deal, especially in a novel with such brilliantly contrary, phenomenological implications. The key is that Chance, building on what he has seen on television, covers his ignorance of what people say to him by the simple habit of repeating parts of their sentences to them, because he thinks "he ought to show a keen interest" in what they say (37). He first tries this ploy on EE; it is a total success: "Each time Chance repeated EE's words, she brightened and looked more confident. In fact, she became so at ease that she began to punctuate her speech by touching, now his shoulder, now his arm" (37). Rand and the President are equally susceptible to Chance's simple little social device. Each man becomes animated when Chance mirrors back the part of himself each has shown the simple man. Chance is seen as a potential lover, a keen businessman, a defender of tight-money, and a cold-war pragmatist for the very natural reason that, in each case, his beholder is (or needs) exactly what he or she sees in Chance. EE is available for him as a lover, Rand has been a powerful businessman, the President himself defends tight money, and Skrapinov must deal with the West.

The characters who are not brain-damaged thus behave in a fashion that is narcissistic in the most basic sense. They look at a blank surface (Chance) and see themselves mirrored there. Like Narcissus, they like what they see. This behavior is certainly flawed, but in a perfectly human and comical way, and not particularly vicious. Clearly it is not pathological. Consequently, it is a form of narcissism that, for the most part, lies outside the basic twentieth-century tradition for discussing such responses—a tradition that, for such examples, seems unnecessarily moralizing and judgmental.

The work that set the tone for discussions of narcissism in this century was Sigmund Freud's 1914 essay "On Narcissism: An Introduction." Here Freud, still working within the Cartesian tradition of strict divisions between subject and object, attempts to distinguish normal love from narcissistic self-love. In normal love, Freud asserts, a subject invests his or her libido in "persons or things in the outer world." This love is object-love. The narcissist, in contrast, does not invest libido primarily in external objects. He (or she) is "a person who treats his own body in the same way as otherwise the body of a sexual object is treated; that is to say, he experiences sexual pleasure in gazing at, caressing and fondling his body, till complete gratification ensues from these activities." As a corollary, Freud associates narcissism with perversion, especially homosexuality. Although conceding that some self-love, "the libidinal complement to the egoism of the instinct of self-preservation, . . . may justifiably be attributed to every living creature," Freud argues that the narcissist *prefers* to love his (or her) ego rather than an external object, that self-love *dominates* the narcissist's choice of objects to love. Freud's position underlies efforts to turn narcissism viewed as pathology into social criticism, the way Christopher Lasch does in *The Culture of Narcissism: American Life in An Age of Diminishing Expectations*.[17]

Admittedly, some of the characteristics that Freud and Lasch call narcissistic show up in Chance and in individuals he encounters outside the garden. Chance is self-protective; that is the reason he is careful to echo what others say to him (37). He relishes the potency and grandiose feelings that come when he watches television: the power to change himself simply by changing channels, the ability to "spread out into the screen without stopping," the sense that he can "bring others inside his eyelids," the belief that he, "and no one else," makes himself be. It flatters him to see that the "figure on the TV screen [looks] like his own reflection in a mirror," that he resembles "the man on TV more than he [differs] from him" (5–6). When offered an opportunity to appear on television, he is "astonished that television [can] portray

17. Sigmund Freud, "On Narcissism: An Introduction," in Freud, *Collected Papers*, trans. Joan Riviere (4 vols.; London, 1934), IV, 30–31, 45; Christopher Lasch, *The Culture of Narcissism: American Life in an Age of Diminishing Expectations* (New York, 1979).

itself," and he looks on the scene with fascination: "Cameras watched themselves and, as they watched, they televised a program. . . . Of all the manifold things there were in all the world . . . only TV constantly held a mirror to its own neither solid nor fluid face" (63).

In the same year that *Being There* appeared, 1971, Henry Malcolm published *Generation of Narcissus,* a book connecting television to narcissism in much the way Kosinski does. Malcolm points out what happens when television becomes a surrogate parent and baby-sitter as it has for many contemporary families: "The child has an experience of learning about reality under the controls of his own will. He can change the channel and—extremely important—walk away from the TV or sit in front of it for hours, play with it and use it in any way that suits his purposes." This power "confirms his narcissistic ego, strengthening it as an instrument for making external reality do what he wants." As a result, rather than struggle with the demands of the external world, "he looks upon traditional demands for social conformity, group psychology, and tribalistic pressure as illegitimate attempts to invade his own universe." His sense of reality, consequently, is more likely to seek "to make reality conform to his needs and wants, than the other way around." Because "television lets the child 'participate' in the world around him long before he has to master the necessary skills . . . required . . . actually to do so . . . many children . . . assume that there is no serious distinction between the world of their own narcissistic egos and the actual outside world." For Malcolm, when such children ultimately confront an external world of "authority, poverty, racism, war, and bureaucracy," one they can no longer change with a flick of the switch, the revelation comes as a shock, leading to serious conflicts.[18]

Much of what Malcolm says in his discussion of television applies directly to Chance, except that Chance never seems to grasp the outward "facts of life" in a way that leads to conflict. He is ultimately more a chameleon in the phenomenological sense than a narcissist. His being-*there* in the world, his low level of need to impose his will on the external world, and his lack of will allow him always to become very much like the world he encounters and so to escape conflict with society.

A few of Chance's other responses to television indicate, however,

18. Henry Malcolm, *Generation of Narcissus* (Boston, 1971), 150–53.

that even in his relatively simple psyche exist conflicts that go much deeper than the social problems Malcolm and Lasch predict for the narcissistic generation.[19] When Chance goes on television, he wants "to see himself reduced to the size of the screen . . . [and] to become an image to dwell inside the set" (60–61). In part, the desire to be reduced repeats the desire for television-validated change he experiences when he switches channels. But this longing may also express the desire for containment of the self he seems to experience when he feels the cameras "licking up the image of his body . . . recording his every movement" (64).

Something deeper, thus, than a desire to change, and less subject to satirical social criticism, is at stake here. For one of the most disturbing symptoms of narcissistic pathology is that the falsely grand self of a narcissist may be extremely fragile and likely to fragment (*AS,* 120). What a narcissist will do to guard against such disintegration may go well beyond Chance's desire for containment and willingness to have his body's image be licked up by cameras. Defenses against disintegration vary from forced activities such as intense physical stimulation, athletic activities, and excessive work to obsessive masturbation, Don Juanism (*AS,* 119), narcissistic rage, and various sadistic or masochistic phantasies and acts (*RS,* 127–28, 194–95). Such defenses against self-fragmentation are, of course, often destructive of the narcissist himself as well as of others.

In Chance's case, his willingness to exhibit himself for the cameras provides no defense. Rather, it overstimulates him, so that even his phantasies of disintegration become grandiose: "The cameras were . . . noiselessly hurling [his every movement] into millions of TV screens scattered throughout the world—into rooms, cars, boats, planes, living rooms, bedrooms. He would be seen by more people than he could ever meet in his entire life—people who would never meet him" (64). At the same time, the experience is surrealistically threatening: "Television reflected only people's surfaces; it also kept peeling their images from their bodies until they were sucked into the caverns of their viewers' eyes, forever beyond retrieval, to disappear" (65).

Although Chance's television appearance in some deep sense validates him as it expands him, it also opens up an old wound. He feels

19. Malcolm, *Generation of Narcissus,* 244–45; Lasch, *Culture of Narcissism,* 103.

that the triple lenses of the camera are like snouts pointed at him and that he has become "only an image for millions of real people" who will "never know how real he [is], since his thinking [can] not be televised" (65). With a more coherent character, one who possessed firmer memories of the past, we would say that this wound is the deepest in Chance's psyche, that it goes back to his parentless infancy and the blow of hearing the Old Man tell him that he is incompetent, illegitimate, and brain-damaged (8). But Chance's emotional wound is not so deep. He quickly covers it by exchanging a few ambiguities about gardening with his television host (65–66), providing one more indication that he ultimately exists in a phenomenological mode rather than a psychological one. Like everything else about him, his narcissism is skin-deep. His interiority is not substantial enough to color his present world significantly, and so he remains a chameleon blending with his setting rather than a narcissist.

The other characters do not share Chance's lack of an interior world. They are unambiguously narcissists, though not always of the sort described by Lasch and Malcolm.

A reader may accept the general disfavor with which Malcolm and especially Lasch greet the emergence of specific narcissistic traits in our culture. But if, like Lasch and many others, we take narcissism as the dominant psychological disorder of the second half of the twentieth century, if we regard narcissism as having replaced the hysteria and the obsessive neuroses that Freud and the early psychoanalysts treated, then, reason and compassion suggest, we must go deeper than Lasch's treatment of narcissism as the target of social criticism.[20] Those, like Lasch, who follow Freud in analyzing narcissism work within what Heinz Kohut calls the "clandestine moral system" that underlies the drive theory of traditional psychoanalysis going back to Freud. Freud's moral assumptions, as summarized by Kohut, are simple: "Drives need to be tamed. People are born uncivilized and need to become civilized."[21]

If we adopt Kohut's less judgmental approach, one that attempts

20. Malcolm, *Generation of Narcissus,* 244–45; Lasch, *Culture of Narcissism,* 74–75, 89; Bennett Simon, *Mind and Madness in Ancient Greece: The Classical Roots of Modern Psychiatry* (Ithaca, 1980), 285–87; *HDAC,* 60–61.

21. Kohut, *Self Psychology,* 221.

"to support human psychological life to its fullest," then we can draw important distinctions between Chance and the lesser characters.[22] First, though, we have to abandon the "erroneous conception" of traditional theory based on Freud's essay "On Narcissism"—the conception that "normal development proceeds from . . . self-love to the love of others" and "from helpless dependence to autonomy." For Kohut, "normality is not tantamount to the claim—the unrealistic claim—that the need for selfobjects [mirroring or idealizable others] is relinquished by the adult and replaced by autonomy and object love." Instead, we will see that narcissism must persist in normal adults, that normal individuals move "from archaic to mature narcissism," that this movement exists "side by side and intertwined with a movement from archaic to mature object love," and that "we do not see an abandonment of self-love and its replacement by the love for others." Neither good health nor maturity requires that we abandon all our relationships of dependency and become "strong and autonomous" or that we turn "self-love into the love of others." Indeed, the need to cling to others and to invest others with self-love may be a healthy indication that the energy required for the self to develop has not been relinquished, that one is still developing, that it is still possible to take full-blooded joy in the presence of others (*HDAC,* 208–209).

From Kohut's new, less-moralizing perspective, traditional social criticism of narcissism seems grandiose, as though it were possible to build a better society without first acknowledging the way one colors the outer world with personal needs and fears and without following the careful discrimination between self and object proposed by Jungians, Kohut, and Freud himself when he writes of examining the archaic drives his patients transferred to the analyst.[23] In opposition to the more modest approach of the analysts, social critiques of narcissism usually imply that the social critic has identified with, or introjected, an idealized authority that causes the critic to judge, without first empathizing with, a group that has come to represent the age.[24] The critics may give the appearance of reason and objectivity, but moralizing judgment traditionally goes hand-in-hand with social criticism

22. *Ibid.,* 221–22.

23. Freud, "On Narcissism," 58–59.

24. *Cf.* Kohut, *Self Psychology,* 197.

and so blocks it from perceiving, in the way Kohut's empathy attempts to perceive, the ultimate nature of its object.[25]

In contrast to the usual critique of narcissism, Kosinski's novel provides a view of contemporary life that is at once critical and empathic. His portrait of Chance shows the protagonist's limitations without having the narrator or the lesser figures judge him harshly, with the exception of the Old Man (8), who may be protecting himself from paternal responsibility. Even Chance's hollowness comes across in a way that creates empathy rather than distance, for most readers have on occasion wanted to appear better informed than they were on subjects beyond their ken. Who does not envy Chance's "wisdom," on such occasions, in choosing silence as the most effective disguise for total ignorance?

Even the narcissists in the novel, who make up the overwhelming majority of the characters (as well as being the normal ones), are dealt with in a comical rather than judgmental fashion. Although they vary from the warmly sympathetic Rands to the scornful chairman of the board of the British Broadcasting Company (BBC) (95) and Chance's ludicrous male "lover" (108–11), they all share a distinguishing trait. They view Chance through a lens colored by their own strengths or needs; they fill his inner vacuum, his lack of projects, with projects of their own.

That this tendency taken by itself is far too human to be judged harshly becomes clear when Kosinski pairs the scene in which a man with "long silky gray hair . . . combed straight from his forehead to the nape of his neck" (107) grotesquely masturbates against the "sole of Chance's shoe" (110) with a parallel one in which EE makes quivering love to her own image of love projected on the blank screen of Chance's "flaccid flesh" (113). She is a healthy sexual woman, and the gray-haired gentleman is homosexual, but they both are narcissistic in the way they view the blankness of Chance. Surely EE is less criticized in her love scene than sexless Chance (77). And if the gray-haired gentleman is treated more harshly than Chance, it is for his fetishism and masochistic groveling rather than for his narcissism.

Kosinski pairs narcissists again in Rand and the President. He handles Rand more gently than he does the President, not because the latter is the more narcissistic but because their motives differ. Much

25. *Ibid.*, 115–16.

the way Chance sees Rand as a substitute for the Old Man (38), the only father he has ever known, so Rand sees Chance as the son from whom he is separated (37, 40), as a young husband for EE after he dies (40), and as his spiritual and financial heir (42). Rand's needs are altogether more sympathetic than those of the President, who uses Chance to back his economic policies (54) and to increase his power with the public (57). Yet both Rand and the President respond to Chance in exactly the same narcissistic fashion: they take his straightforward comments as agrarian metaphors (40, 54).

The President is also paired, politically this time, with Soviet ambassador Skrapinov, who reads Chance's literal remark about their chairs almost touching as a metaphor for the coexistence of American capitalism and Soviet marxism (89). This misreading serves Skrapinov as well in his struggles with "the geese," probably the masses, as the President's misreading serves him with the American public.

Kosinski additionally plays Skrapinov off against the boys in the backroom from the President's party. Whereas Skrapinov first sees Chance as a man who shares his "down-to-earth philosophy" (89), the boys who plan to nominate Chance for high office are most attracted by his blank past, his lack of a background or a record, an absence they can package as the innocence the American public expects from candidates (138–39).

Representation of the American nostalgia for innocence may be Kosinski's most far-reaching yet indirect statement about narcissism. For in the same way that the Soviets are flattered by the appearance of down-to-earthness, so the American voters are pleased by an empty mirror of their own lost innocence. These appearances so flatter both societies that entire nations are blinded by mere mirrors of what they nostalgically seek to be again: little more than unthinking consciousnesses of pleasing images caught in the mirror of the age, the television screen.

The character who comes nearest to criticizing the public directly for its blindness is BBC board chairman Lord Beauclerk, who appears in only two paragraphs. He takes Chance's brief statement during his television appearance, which actually consists of truisms about gardens and the seasons, as having been both blunt and cunning, as well as properly contemptuous of the videots who watch (95). He goes further than Kosinski, though, in casting stones at the mob. For Kosinski as novelist can hardly be ignorant either of the way fictions are fashioned from the novelist's own narcissistic investments of personal strengths and foibles in characters or of the way a novel depends on the reader's taking the book as a glass in which he or she sees images of the conscious and unconscious dimensions of the self. A novel about narcissism has to be written with a kind of empathy, and therefore modesty, which is lacking in the BBC executive, who sees in Chance another sacrificial god like himself to be punished by an infirm public (95).

The executive's transcendence belongs to the pure consciousness of the social critic, not to the imagination of the novelist, who must be implicated in the infirmities of every character he or she expects to come to life in the reader's mirrored mind. The phenomenological tradition that runs from Husserl, through Heidegger and Sartre, to Chance may or may not support legitimate social criticism. Kosinski as novelist, however, belongs to the tradition of creative narcissism that, because it begins in the energy of the psyche itself, underlies, without regard to time or place, the urge of the imagination to unfold.

V Men and Women Under the Myth: John Barth's *Chimera*

The models of behavior we have observed thus far, both Protean and narcissistic types, come together for brilliant dramatic contrast in John Barth's *Chimera,* published in 1972. Because these extremes of behavior do not satisfy Barth, however, he employs his remarkable imaginative powers to create alternatives to Proteus and Narcissus.

Such dissatisfaction and originality should be familiar to Barth's readers, for surely he is our most inventive contemporary American novelist. He may also be our most creative and, if we consider his contributions to postmodernism, our most influential. Among the themes developed in his complex trilogy of tales, *Chimera,* the opposition between Protean characters and those with a fixed destiny may not, at first, appear as important as other subjects treated, including the competition between the sexes and the nature of storytelling. Yet Barth's contrast of character types serves a central purpose, for it helps bring together the other, more obvious topics. At the same time, because the contrast is not the foreground of the book, using it for focus gives the reader a place to stand in responding to *Chimera* and a perspective a degree freer of Barth's own metafictional commentary that, by preempting discussion of the overt themes, tends to dominate readings of the book.

A position outside Barth's commentary can be helpful, for Barth's meanings often lie hidden beneath his brilliant surfaces. The great modernist texts of Eliot, Joyce, and Pound employed the tortured beauty of fragments, ellipses, and associative syntax to bypass the censors, both personal and social, while exploring otherwise unthinkable sexual and social issues important to the early century. In the same way, Barth employs convoluted phantasies and metafictions in the style of postmodernism to open the mind to problems of the late twentieth century that readers might otherwise prefer to deny. To put the censors at ease, he removes his tales from the moralized, canonical myths of our era and focuses on noncanonical myths of the ancient Middle East. His ploy sets him free to play, to explore, to revise our mythology as his inward urges insist, a process that leads to healing discoveries about the roles men and women play in an age when the feminist revolution has put the underlying myth of our culture in question.

The contrast between Protean and fixed characters in *Chimera* is what the reader should expect from the novelist who, when he created Henry Burlingame as a central figure in *The Sot-Weed Factor* in 1960, pioneered the exploration in contemporary American literature of Protean freedom, after Ralph Ellison's Rinehart and Saul Bellow's Augie March, with Herman Melville's Confidence Man and James Weldon Johnson's Ex-Colored Man as distant predecessors. In *The Sot-Weed Factor,* Burlingame explains himself to his opposite number, Ebenezer Cooke, whose fixed identity is that of virgin and poet: "Your true and constant Burlingame lives only in your fancy. . . . In fact you see a Heraclitean flux: whether 'tis we who shift and alter and dissolve; or you whose lens changes color, field, and focus; or both together." Barth had moved steadily toward this clear opposition of character types in his two earlier novels, when he played absurdist Todd Andrews against chameleonlike Harrison Mack in *The Floating Opera,* published in 1956, and self-canceling Jacob Horner against dangerously consistent Joe Morgan in *The End of the Road,* which came out in 1958.[1] After Burlingame, the clear contrast appeared a second time in *Giles Goat-Boy; or, The Revised New Syllabus* in 1966, where George Giles, destined to be the Grand Tutor, struggles against shape-shifting Harold Bray. This opposition of types, therefore, may be the central conflict of Barth's books, certainly of his early ones.

Two years after *Giles Goat-Boy,* the opposition reemerged in several

1. John Barth, *The Sot-Weed Factor* (New York, 1964), 204–205, 349; John Barth, *The Floating Opera* (New York, 1956), 28–29, 49–50; John Barth, *The End of the Road* (New York, 1969), 67–68, 152–55.

short pieces in *Lost in the Funhouse,* published in 1968. In "Echo," Barth contrasts the beautiful youth Narcissus, who obsessively denies "all except himself," with sad Echo, who effaces "herself absolutely." Narcissus' dogged pursuit of self causes him to languish away by the mirroring pool. Echo's self-effacing allows her to survive, but only as the Protean repetition of others' voices. In Barth's interpretation, the opposite types "come to the same" end, for "it was never himself Narcissus craved, but his reflection," his visual echo. Because "his self-knowledge . . . persists, persists" in Echo's voice, "his death must be [only a] partial" death, as Echo's self-less life can only be a partial life. Both Narcissus and Echo, Beverly Bienstock argues, represent the situation of an author. Characters mirror their creator's natural narcissism, and an author's work echoes the voices, and lives, of its characters. But the life, even the immortality, the author gains thereby is only a partial life.[2] Consequently, as late as "Echo," no exit from the dilemma represented by narcissism and Proteanism seemed available for Barth's characters.

In the same book, Barth carried the freedom afforded by Protean variability to its alphabetical extreme in the obsessive "Life-Story." There, an author who one afternoon considers "that his own life might be a fiction, in which he [is] the leading or an accessory character," goes on for a dozen pages to become one letter (*C*?) in a literal alphabet of narrators, *A* to *Z,* all of them writing stories about other authors while trying to escape an (alphabetically) earlier narrator's fiction.[3] Presumably, if the process continued, narrator Z would be, in Barth's recurring Möbius fashion, the author of A's story, so that the cycle could twist upon itself and continue. Even though none of the authors seems to care for such artifice-acknowledging fictions, none can go back to writing straightforward mimetic tales.

Barth's infinite regress of narrators appears to be an inevitability not only of twentieth-century literature's commitment to self-consciousness but also of twentieth-century philosophy. Here Edmund Husserl's phenomenological ideal of the transcendental ego—an ideal that has been a mainstay, as we have seen, of twentieth-century

2. John Barth, *Lost in the Funhouse* (Garden City, N.Y., 1968), 102–103; Beverly Gray Bienstock, "Lingering on the Autognostic Verge: John Barth's *Lost in the Funhouse,*" *Modern Fiction Studies,* XIX (Spring, 1973), 77–78.

3. Barth, *Lost in the Funhouse,* 116.

culture especially after purification into Sartre's existential consciousness called "Being-for-itself"—finds its literary incarnation in the device of framing stories. Authors who transcend the swamp of their earlier life by making that past a fiction of which they are the author have discovered a convenient device for liberating "Being-for-itself." They seek the anguish of existential freedom to escape the nausea of a defined identity, of being bogged down in the story of one's past. At the same time, they remain true to Alain Robbe-Grillet's proposition that the purpose of contemporary fiction is to lead the way to imaginative freedom by showing how one invents the work and, thereby, the world and one's own life.[4]

In avoiding the nausea of fixed identity, however, "Life-Story" dramatizes the malaise of phenomenology. Although the situation, an alphabet soup of narrators, is absurd and suitable for satire or parody, the tone nonetheless has the resonance of heartfelt parody. The shape-shifting of the narrator from identity to alphabetical identity becomes frenzied. His need never to be controlled by an externally determined or authored self leads to a flood of fears—fears of abstract formalism, of fantasy, distortion, fragmentation, obsession, eventually of schizophrenia and suicide.[5] Protean freedom is one thing, Protean fragmentation another altogether. Here the line between the two is easily blurred. Indeed, the distance between high-spirited Henry Burlingame and the troubled narrator of "Life-Story" is much less than the 280 years that separate them would imply. The act of connecting the two in the reader's imagination draws a reasonably straight line through Barth's Möbius-turned universe.

The distance between the "Life-Story" narrator and the prehistoric Greek Polyeidus in *Chimera* is even shorter, and yet not less than that between Bellerophon, intent on becoming a mythical Greek hero, and Ebenezer Cooke or George Giles, each with his sense of destiny. Bellerophon and Polyeidus represent the most obvious developments in *Chimera* of Barth's pattern of playing fixed characters against Protean figures, but other characters, male and female, in the three novellas provide clarifying variations of the contrast.

In "Perseid," for example, Barth opposes the narrow rigidity of An-

4. Alain Robbe-Grillet, *For a New Novel: Essays on Fiction,* trans. Richard Howard (New York, 1965), 156.

5. Barth, *Lost in the Funhouse,* 118, 124.

dromeda to the flexible constancy of Medusa and plays petrifying, middle-aged Perseus off against his younger heroic self. In "Bellerophoniad," the varied contrasts include the imitative Anteia and one-dimensional Philonoe opposed to the multidimensioned Melanippe, as well as role-dominated Bellerophon/Deliades set against shape-shifting Polyeidus. In "Dunyazadiad," the culminating tale, though placed first for the publisher's misguided commercial reasons, Barth plays off a Faustian Scheherazade against her sister Dunyazade, who remains her own woman; the tale also frames the one-role Shahryar with the more complex Shah Zaman.[6] In addition, "Dunyazadiad" offers the passionate Genie to contrast as an author to the mutable and self-effacing Polyeidus and the imitative Jerome B. Bray of "Bellerophoniad."

For all these characters except Polyeidus and Bray, gender roles present major problems. Central to gender roles is the myth of the hero so brilliantly stated and developed in "Perseid," the first of the tales Barth wrote.[7] Perseus' problem sounds the obvious theme of the three-part novel: how are men and women ever to transcend the myth of heroic maleness that, "Bellerophoniad" reminds us, has dominated Western culture since the overthrow of the matriarchy some 3,500 years ago.[8] Although asserted by Anteia, a flawed, generally satirized character, the existence of a matriarchy prior to the emergence of Homer's Mycenaean heroes accords with modern historical reconstructions of the eastern Mediterranean, especially following Spyridon Marinatos' excavations of Akrotiri on the Greek island of Thera, which show the role the Thera eruptions played in destroying the Minoan civilization and opening the way for the Mycenaeans. Artifacts in the National Archeological Museum in Iraklion, Crete, reveal the overthrow of the older earth goddesses of the matriarchy by the younger sky gods of the patriarchy, who were led by Zeus and are closely tied to the Western heroic myth.[9]

As the son of Zeus and the princess Danae, Perseus may originally

6. David Morrell, *John Barth: An Introduction* (University Park, Pa., 1976), 162.

7. *Ibid.*, 140–43.

8. John Barth, *Chimera* (New York, 1972), 277; hereinafter cited parenthetically by page number in the text.

9. William H. McNeill, *The Rise of the West: A History of the Human Community* (New York, 1963), 109–28; Emily Vermeule, *Greece in the Bronze Age* (Chicago, 1972), 155 n. Anteia's claim that the matriarchy was "the original and natural" order of things,

have taken to the heroic part naturally enough. David Morrell is correct, therefore, in saying that Perseus is "his own man finally."[10] From the start, however, Perseus seems benighted; his heroic behavior arises from a great reservoir of unconsciousness. His eagerness in middle life to feel heroic again suggests that the heroic pattern is the only masculine role he knows or feels comfortable playing (91).

Whatever its source in Perseus' life, the myth serves useful purposes. The way he ponders the murals in Calyxa's temple indicates that the pattern lends meaning, an external one, to a demigod's life (80–81). His anxiety that his cousin Bellerophon may challenge his greatness in Athene's eyes implies that the heroic role helps satisfy his masculine need to feel special (93). This specialness, as his relationships with Athene, Calyxa, Andromeda, and especially Medusa (who loved her beheader) demonstrate, is a feeling that not only Perseus but perhaps all heroes acquire from the way women respond to their heroic feats (87–88, 90, 93).

The dependency of heroes on the impressionability of women combines with Perseus' recurring anxieties about his sexual potency and the size of his organ (66, 68–70) to suggest a very modern explanation for an ancient pattern of behavior: that heroic role-playing compensates for deepseated sexual anxieties by enabling heroes to deny their anxieties. Barth draws some of his best comedy from such anachronistic connections that would have been as unthinkable in a heroic shame culture as in a modern locker room or barracks. When Calyxa asks Perseus if he is "really so naive as to equate love-making, like a callow lad, with mere prolonged penetration," he replies twice: "Yes. 'I'm a *hero!*' I indicated with a sweep of my relieved glories [the murals], whose first extension she had revealed to me that day. 'Virtuoso performance is my line of work!'" (70). Perseus' anxiety here cannot be altogether a product of his midlife crisis, for even if potency was not a problem of his youthful heroic cycle, it is still unlikely that his member has shrunk during the intervening years. Thus, like Napoleon, he has had something to compensate for for a long time.

---

however, makes no allowance for the hunting culture of the much older cave dwellers around the great central sea.

10. Morrell, *John Barth,* 152.

In this playful manner, even in the most heroic and most sympathetic to males of the three novellas, Barth has begun his exploration of weaknesses that hide behind the myth of maleness. Because Perseus' heroic behavior is in part compensatory, a way to deny anxieties, it belongs to a dimension of the demigod's self that is largely a pretense and therefore false. As a result, even when the hero succeeds in fooling women with his heroism, he feels the pretense in himself. In this manner the heroic pattern generates its own form of anxiety. Perseus, for example, has spent "years of comparative study" attempting to determine whether his "post-Medusan years [were] an example of or an exception to the archetypal pattern for heroic adventure" (80). He may have succeeded in selling his heroic role to the Calyxas and the Medusas of the prehistoric Middle East, but in moments of self-doubt he is the first to admit that "no man's a mythic hero to his wife" (87). The wife it is who most sees through the heroic pretense and assesses the flawed man (or demigod) beneath the marble mask. For long years Andromeda has been house-training and henpecking her rescuer and onetime hero (76). Both Perseus and Calyxa consider the possibility that Andromeda has henpecked him into his present psychosexual weakness (76, 87). Yet the anxiety about size must surely antedate both Andromeda and the heroic feats.

Some of Perseus' psychosexual difficulty, however, appears to be situational, the product of a mixed marriage, Argive and Ethiopian (77), man and woman. For Andromeda has nailed home to Perseus a truth that is anathema to the myth of the hero: "that a woman's a person in her independent right, to be respected therefor by the goldenest hero in heaven" (76). Her ceaseless struggle for parity has taken the starch out of Perseus' stiff image of himself as hero and, in the process, has wrecked the marriage (77). The limper Perseus' self-confidence has grown, the more rigid Andromeda, daughter of a similarly dominating mother (76), has turned. As Perseus sees their relationship, "the more she became her own woman, the less" she was his (85). In their second cycle's final encounter, all she wants, she claims, is "to build as best she [can] a life of her own," alone (125). Unfortunately for Perseus, even the worshipful Calyxa, in Barth's updating of the myth, enjoys her "free, independent life" and recognizes that, as much as she adores her hero, they "don't really relate" and so would "probably drive each other crazy if [they] stayed together" (109). Even she cannot offer Perseus heaven on earth. The situation between men and women appears to be all oil and vinegar, especially when, as Andromeda points out, the male is a mythic hero with an "insufferable ego" that proposes "three parts Perseus to one Andromeda" (77).

If in his first cycle Perseus passionately pursued the fixed destiny of the heroic myth, he learns here in his second cycle the necessity of incorporating an opposite sort of behavior: to "proceed . . . with neither armor nor disguise"; *not* to cut off Medusa's head; to recognize "he's not the only golden hero in Greece"; to share the winged horse Pegasus with the new hero Bellerophon; to "endure with patience [the] threats and insults" of the hideous Graeae; and to assist them in recovering their missing eye (92–93). In short, his "mode of operation in this second enterprise must be contrary to [his] first's": it must be "direct instead of indirect" and "rather passive than active" (93–94). "Beyond a certain point [he] must permit things to come to [him] instead of adventuring to them" (94). Such behavior, of course, has little place in the heroic pattern.

Nor is Perseus' new behavior, "beyond a certain point," part of the traditional male pattern, which was, according to Jungian analyst Robert Johnson, to go on a quest, to initiate action. The woman's role, in contrast, was to wait for extraordinary events to come to her.[11] From Johnson's perspective, Perseus, in the second half of his life, has to develop the other half of his personality, the so-called feminine traits, so that he can become something more than the marble facade he became as a Greek hero. In his second cycle, he is required to become less heroic and more perfectly human.

This mandate comes from the hooded woman who visits him in *Nao Athinis,* the Temple of Athene (94), bearing the wisdom of his half-sister Athene (93), whose surrogate he takes her to be (90). His instructress, as he later discovers, is Medusa herself, and her goal is to steer him toward his deeper humanity so that finally, through mutual commitment, they may together become immortal stars.

If Medusa is Athene's surrogate, she is also Andromeda's antithesis. Though Andromeda later claims she loved "Perseus the man" (124), she has dealt with Perseus chiefly in his heroic roles, as both golden rescuer and has-been, each of which she obviously resents (77–78). In

11. Robert Johnson, *She,* 41.

contrast, Medusa seeks a Perseus with an expanded repertoire of behavior.

Medusa, too, has known the hero and in an ambivalent manner has, like Andromeda, been rescued by him. For, as she tells her story, her rape by Poseidon in Athene's temple, together with Athene's punishment, had doomed her to the coldness of Hyperborea (the far north). There she dwelt with the hideous Gorgons, those "snakehaired frights" the sight of whom "was enough to turn Medusa's suitors to stone when they approached her" (89). In Medusa's telling, she never knows whether she herself has a Gorgon's head, but the chance she might "be as Gorgon as her sisters" makes her welcome decapitation by Perseus as deliverance from the coldness to which ravishment by Poseidon has doomed her (90). In emotional terms, Perseus' arrival unwittingly frees her from the cold, man-petrifying rage that followed her rape. Medusa strangely awaited the coming of Perseus as "a golden dream" (90).

The myth of Medusa, told from her point of view, thus lends a far different meaning to Perseus' bloody deed and to Medusa's life. It shows that beneath the role Medusa played as Perseus' monster-victim lives a complex woman. As Perseus claims, she is both his "true adversary and chief ally," not because beheading her made him famous, as he once thought (78), but because their stories are linked in ways he originally did not recognize. Because her true identity is veiled from Perseus, the narrator, the coherence of her personality easily escapes the reader.

As Perseus was Medusa's unwitting rescuer, she is his unrecognized guide through the second cycle of his life. It is she, her face hidden by a hood, who advises the shipwrecked hero when he consults Athene in the goddess' temple on Seriphos (84, 86), she who over the years instructs Calyxa regarding scenes to include in the marble murals of his life (86), she who informs him that the purpose of his second cycle is to become a new Perseus by learning restraint and undoing the heroic damage of his early life (93–94). It is Medusa also who, having led Perseus from Athene's temple to the courtyard, willingly submits her "ample soft young body, wide-hipped and small-breasted," to Perseus' anxiety-ridden embraces of a woman whose face he has never seen (94–95). At the crisis of his second cycle, it is Medusa who waits at the bottom of Lake Triton to save him from drowning (97–98), resuscitates him (99), and reminds him that Athene requires he return the Graeae their eye "at once, unconditionally" (99), in short, that he relinquish his heroic cunning and act forthrightly.

Having saved Perseus again from despair, Medusa asks a series of questions about his quest for rejuvenation, queries reinterpreted by Calyxa as the riddle crucial to his later life: "How can Being Perseus Again be your goal, when you have to be Perseus to reach it?" (100). It is a mystery that goes beyond the goal-directed behavior of heroes, a paradox no hero can be expected to understand or answer, for it distinguishes being from doing: a hero comprehends but one thing, the willful action that a quest creates. For him, that action is the single mode of being that has value. Everything else belongs to a malaise, the boredom of waiting for the quest.

Medusa underscores Perseus' heroic blindness when she lets him make love to her again (100–101). Ironically, this act occurs amid the suicidal despair he falls into when the Graeae refuse to tell him how once again to find the Styx-Nymphs, whose equipment he needed in his first cycle to defeat Medusa (63, 96, 99). Because he does not comprehend that Medusa, the goal of his quest, is already at hand, his pursuit of Perseus-like heroism has again blinded him to the human Perseus whom Medusa sees, loves (106–107), and patiently assists into being. He has confused a role, heroism, which should be a means to an end, with a state of being, loving Medusa, which should be an end in itself.

Perseus spends the remainder of his tale coming to terms with his ambivalence about Andromeda (110–11, 120, 125) and realizing that estellation, endless stardom, requires not heroic action but restraint and committed loving. He must decide whether he loves Medusa enough to satisfy a condition the goddess of wisdom has placed on Medusa's revealing her face: if his love runs deep enough to accept the possible Gorgon head, "the two of them [will] turn ageless as the stars and be together forever" (107). The extent of his growth becomes clear when, having figuratively slain the "young Perseus," his double, by clobbering his half-brother and Andromeda's new lover, Danaus (122–23), he sufficiently masters his heroic vanity to forgo murdering the raging Andromeda and, in the same heartbeat, embraces "the paradoxic precious" Medusa (125). Just as Medusa was a constant but invisible audience from the first words ("Good evening") of his nightly retelling of his tale, so through the second cycle of his life she is both an invisible guiding presence and waiting goal, his future already present, because she has loved him constantly since his heroic past (105).

Medusa, or her spirit, is also felt as an invisible presence in the other two novellas. Clearly, Bellerophon seeks his own Medusa in Melanippe, and even though Dunyazade is the primary narrator of her own tale rather than primary audience, as were Medusa and Melanippe, she is the spiritual heir (or progenitor, depending on which direction one moves along the Möbius-strip chronology) of Medusa. In each case, the Medusa figure offers the chief positive alternative to the dominant myth of masculine heroism. Medusa-like qualities that recur in the other figures include an inner vision that leads to constant goals, a measure of flexibility, and remarkable powers of empathy, even extending to monsters and adversaries (127).

Medusa and Perseus have one distinct advantage over their parallels in "Bellerophoniad." As Perseus tells her in their eternal epilogue, "At the time we were archetypes, not stereo types; reality, not myth" (129). Only in his second cycle does Perseus "wish his time turned back" (133) so that he can relive his heroic youth, and the second cycle eventually brings him the wisdom to put that "unpleasant middle Perseus . . . to death . . . forever" (124). Even when he tries to imitate his youthful self, the attempt itself springs from a spontaneous need within the aging man.

Not so Bellerophon. His effort to recycle his earlier life is part of a conscious, lifelong imitation of the heroic pattern, especially as he, on his fortieth birthday, finds it set forth in the story of Perseus, his model hero (137–38). When we discover that Bellerophon is in fact Deliades (306), we see that, as with Perseus, the need to behave in a heroic manner is at base a grandiose compensation for underlying inferiority. In the case of Bellerophon/Deliades, inferiority comes not from Perseus-like anxiety about penis size but from playing second fiddle to Bellerus, who their mother Eurymede claimed was Poseidon's son, a "demigod destined for the stars" (151). Having begun life "circumspect, prudential," moderate, and wise (151), Deliades became his brother's "mortal killer" and buried himself under the name "Bellerophon" (the voice, or murderer, of Bellerus) "to live out in selfless counterfeit, from that hour to this, [his] brother's demigoddish life" (306), thus creating a myth not of heroism but of role-playing, of the counterfeit life, of inauthenticity.

The significance of Bellerophon's myth and of *Chimera* itself is clearly that "by imitating perfectly the Pattern of Mythic Heroism, [one becomes], not a mythic hero, but a perfect Reset [*i.e.,* an imitation of the Pattern of Mythic Heroism]" (303). That is the fate of Bellerophon, would have been the fate of Perseus had Medusa not been his constant guide, and would have been the fate of Shah Zaman had he not had Dunyazade as audience and had he not possessed inner resources not visible in his public role of heroic (that is, compensatory) manhood.

Bellerophon/Deliades shares his fate with his father, Polyeidus. As Bellerophon finally recognizes, "only Polyeidus's son could have mimed a life so well, so long" (306). Inasmuch as Polyeidus is not a demigod or a hero—at most he is the mere verbal and pictorial pattern of the hero's life (260–61)—Barth through Polyeidus indicates that imitation of the received role of male heroism is only part, if a significant part, of a larger problem: the counterfeit life that one takes from the external world rather than spins from the central self. Polyeidus, whose name means "many shapes," is Barth's most Protean character, excepting Proteus himself in "Menelaiad" from *Lost in the Funhouse*. However, whereas Proteus turned, in his daughter's words, "first into animals, then into plants and wine-dark sea, then into no saying what," Polyeidus, as though captured by Professor Henry Higgins or a contemporary French critic, turns, as he becomes increasingly self-conscious, into mere words, documents epistolary, literary, or historical (152–53).[12] In his final identity as the intentionally botched mock epic "Bellerophoniad," he becomes, like Barth's Echo, an anonymous grouping of "false letters" that spell out his imitative son's tale.

The fate of father and son here is a far cry from the fate of Perseus and Medusa, who became "these silent, visible signs," stars and words, which are meant "to *be* the tale [Perseus tells] to those with eyes to see and understanding to interpret; to raise [Medusa] up forever and know that [Perseus' and Medusa's] story will never be cut off, but nightly rehearsed as long as men and women read the stars" (133–34). In contrast to the exhilaration the reader feels with "Perseid," the reader of "Bellerophoniad" can scarcely wait to finish and move on to the next story, or, if he has read them in the unfortunate order imposed

12. Barth, *Lost in the Funhouse,* 160.

by the publisher, recycle the novellas by turning back to "Dunyazadiad."

Impatience with "Bellerophoniad" does not mean that the tale fails to do what Barth asks of it, only that it functions far less effectively as an ending than as the middle of a fiction. It introduces new characters who help fill the wide gap between extremes found throughout Barth's works that play Protean characters against those with a fixed destiny. At the same time it develops themes stated in "Perseid" by introducing figures who clarify the opposition between role-players like middle Perseus and characters who, like Medusa and the final Perseus, remain who they are.

Such integrity of character is a difficult concept to treat in postmodern fiction, for the age is largely phenomenological and postmoralistic. The heritage of phenomenology, especially through Sartrean existentialism, has stressed Being as discontinuous moments of consciousness of objects. A consistent self is more and more viewed as a construct (a fiction) of reflexive consciousness. One's essence is said to be what one has been, one's past. Each man, like Proteus, "makes his essence as he lives."[13] At the same time, the postmodern period inherits the antimoralizing stance of the New Criticism that John Crowe Ransom derived from I. A. Richards, T. S. Eliot, William Empson, and other early-twentieth-century theorists. From this perspective, an author who stresses integrity of character might easily appear didactic.

Barth avoids both problems. No contemporary author, with the possible exception of Pynchon, has created characters more Protean than Barth's Henry Burlingame, Harold Bray, Proteus, and Polyeidus. Yet Barth does not embrace such figures enthusiastically, the way a committed phenomenologist would. His shape-shifters may not seem simpletons like his characters who pursue a fixed destiny, Ebenezer Cooke, George Giles, and Bellerophon; but a comparison of Polyeidus and Bellerophon, variable father and simple son, reveals that the two sets of characters are alike in one fatal way. They are all role-players. Whether they pursue an abstract role, like those who set out toward a certain destiny, or whether, Proteus-like, they assume a seemingly boundless series of parts, all conform to externals. Like phenomenological man, each Barthian shape-shifter lives a decentered exis-

13. Sartre, *Being and Nothingness,* 630.

tence. Indeed, in Sartre's persuasive ontology, the concept of a center makes no sense, except as bad faith, as self-deception. Despite Sartre's brilliant exposition, though, Barth presents in *Chimera,* quietly, with no didactic flourishes and in an understated fashion, a group of characters, including Medusa, Melanippe, Dunyazade, even the men Shah Zaman and the Genie/author, who appear to act from a constant center without assuming grandiose roles.

Melanippe, for example, stands in stark contrast to Anteia and, less starkly, to Philonoe. In a sense, both Melanippe and Anteia are seduced by the male heroic myth, but their reasons are very different, Melanippe's largely cultural, Anteia's narrowly personal. Having been captured and raped by Bellerophon (216), Melanippe with justifiable anger recounts her cultural myth of the descent of the Amazons "from a company of some two thousand virgins forcibly deflowered by an Asian despot who then transported them en masse to Scythia," where "they established a militant gynocracy to oppose the forcible suppression of their sex" (218). Anteia mirrors Bellerophon in that a longing for personal grandiosity, which she associates with gods and heroes, creates her need to mate with a god or demigod (174), a desire that expresses her cross-sexual wish "to be a mythic hero" (180). Hers is the risible penis envy produced by a culture in which it is not men but only heroes who behave in ways the culture is conditioned to value. Anteia, as much as Perseus and Bellerophon, falls victim to the appeal of the heroic pattern. Her longing turns her into a grotesque parody of male heroism when she becomes not the king she wants to be but the "queen" of the new absolute matriarchy of Tiryns. "Now about fifty, heavy-set and light-mustached," she is intent on castrating Bellerophon (275) and rewriting the "great body of our classic myths" that support "the myth of heroic maleness." Her revised mythology will obviously serve the vanity of female supremists as effectively as old myths served male supremists (277–78). Anteia may thus be an Aristotelian pendulum swing away from Bellerophon, but she is, like him, a role-playing imitation of the pattern of the mythic hero.

Anteia's sister Philonoe seems a harmless, simple individual, always supportive of and faithful to her husband Bellerophon (139) no matter how selfishly he tries her loyalty. Before Philonoe met Bellerophon, she was a student of mythology, a perceptive, articulate young woman, to judge from remarks her husband repeats (208–209). Criticizing an innocent such as Philonoe may seem as unfair as scoffing at the innocent foolishness of Richard Wagner's Parsifal. There is, however, something at once self-abnegating and patronizing in the way she defers to Bellerophon as a hero (208). In determining her role in the tale, her name may provide a clue, for while the literal translations, "kindly mind" or "loving to think" (*philo-noeo*), provide little help, substituting Husserl's term *noesis* ("the intentional direction by consciousness toward an object external to it") very nearly sums up Philonoe's character.[14] She is one of those women, so pitied in our age, who appear to "love" directing all their time and energy toward an external object, a husband or child or both. Although such dutiful wifeliness may arise from deep-seated inner needs, it remains a role taken from the external world, not from within. Philonoe, as she admits, has grown "dull and uninteresting . . . just at the time when [her husband and marriage most need] a spot of perking up" (236). Self-neglect and sacrifice for her husband have led to her unfortunate state.

In contrast to Philonoe and Anteia, Melanippe maintains her center no matter what role or roles she plays. Like Anteia, she is an Amazon (146), but a lifelong Amazon, not a midlife convert. Like Polyeidus, she is a shape-shifter with "a kind of limited Protean capacity," but only "when sexually in extremis" (215). Despite this Protean quality and the Amazon behavior that comes to her, like her name ("one of a dozen-odd given names" the Amazons use), as a cultural role, Melanippe lives from a center: "For distinct from her 'Melanippe self' [her cultural role] . . . Melanippe knows a private, un-categorizable self impossible for her ever to confuse with the name *Melanippe*—as Perseus, she believes, confused himself with the mythical persona *Perseus,* Bellerophon *Bellerophon*" (238). Even as "the only true Amazon in a courtful of falsies," she "feels herself to be by no means comprehended by that epithet" (237). For she is herself, a category of one that fits her better, she believes, than even the two categories "human being, female" (237).

This private self gives her the energy to reject Bellerophon's effort to impose a Medusa-like role on her as the audience of his tale. In the long first part of "Bellerophoniad," when Bellerophon attempts to wrap his tale up with a "Perseid"-like ending depicting himself and Melanippe enjoying their love as it "winds through universal space and time and all" (291), she interrupts his borrowed daydream: "I can't

14. *Ibid.*, 632.

believe you wrote this mess. . . . It's a lie! It's false! It's full of holes!" (291). The protest that follows seems to come from her heart: "I'm tired of Amazoning; I'm tired of being a demigod's girlfriend. . . . What I want is a plain ordinary groovy husband and ten children, nine of them boys" (293). The myth of matriarchy satisfies the inward Melanippe as little as did the myth of patriarchy.

This profound sense of self ironically earns her her name in the trilogy. Whatever *melanippe* ("dark mare") may have meant to Amazons, a dark horse to modern readers is an unexpected winner, a metaphor that, in a literary context, might signify that a character's function or value has been carefully understated. As a dark horse, she is a Medusa figure, for in "Perseid" Medusa's importance was similarly played down. Yet both women emerge as the characters who best exemplify a self that is centered, constant but flexible, and capable of initiating concerted action. Understatement with Melanippe again permits Barth, without becoming didactic, to represent integrity to an age intrigued by Protean variability.

The title character of "Dunyazadiad" serves a similar purpose. Dunyazade, who for much of the story seems a mere passive reporter of events, ultimately stands in bold contrast to Shahryar and her sister Scheherazade and in shaded contrast to Shahryar's brother Shah Zaman. At the same time, she receives surprising thematic reenforcement from the Genie/author.

The overt power of *Chimera*'s true conclusion comes from Scheherazade who, Faust-like, puts on in turn the disciplines of knowledge her age provides, politics, psychology, mythology, and folklore, in an impassioned effort "to stop Shahryar from killing [a virgin every night] and wrecking the country" (5–7). With good reason, Sherry has been swallowed by her hatred of Shahryar (21) and the view that relations between men and women rest on coercion and deception (19). Driven to outrage, she tells her little sister: "The only pleasure I'll take in [Shahryar's] bed is the pleasure of saving my sisters and cuckolding their killer" (21). At the climax of the tale, she instructs her sister to act, after their double weddings, as she will act: geld her husband, choke him with his own genitals, then slit her own throat (38). The grandiosity of Scheherazade's righteous white rage very nearly consumes them all.

Dunyazade, however, has from the early days of their scheme

sensed the one-dimensional quality of the hatred her sister expresses, the ambivalence of Scheherazade's relationship to Shahryar. When she watches their sexual confrontations, she thinks, "I couldn't tell whether her outcries were of pain, surprise, or—mad as the notion seemed—a kind of pleasure despite herself" (21). Dunyazade, whose knowledge of sex is encyclopedic but secondhand, borrowed from "all the manuals of love and erotic stories in Sherry's library" (21), makes an important distinction when she fully realizes that what she witnesses between her sister and their adversary is, "not conjured illustrations from those texts, but things truly taking place" (22). The obvious distinction here is between the literary and the real. The covert distinction, however, in the context of Sherry's possible pleasure despite herself, is one between deliberate hatred of Shahryar and an unacknowledged tie to the king. This repressed feeling for the man returns to Sherry's conscious life at the end of both "Dunyazadiad" and *The Stories of the Thousand Nights and a Night* when the two "royal couples—Shahryar and Scheherazade, Shah Zaman and Dunyazade—emerge from their bridal chambers after the wedding night, greet one another with warm good mornings," and relinquish their rigid social roles of tyrants and victim-rebels to become joint authors of the book in which they appear (55). Scheherazade's shift here signifies that her behavior to this point has been an assumed role, not the complete expression of needs at her core. She has been under the spell of a social and sexual role.

The same may be said of Shahryar and Shah Zaman. Like the middle Perseus and Bellerophon, they are, as the Genie/author suggests, deranged by a spell (22)—the spell of the male myth. For Perseus, the male myth of the hero compensated for his imagined organ inferiority. For Bellerophon/Deliades, it covered an imagined inferiority to his brother Bellerus. For the two kings in this climactic tale of *Chimera,* the myth of male heroic superiority is the way men save face, the way Shah Zaman, for example, keeps from seeming "chicken-hearted and a fool" (55) or, worst yet, from seeming a cuckold.

This tale, which penetrates furthest into causes of the grandiose myth of male heroic power, indicates that men set themselves up as patriarchs with life-and-death control over women to compensate for an ultimate powerlessness. Central to the tale and to the whole of *Chimera* is the early story, Sherry's favorite, of the "ifrit who steals a girl away on her wedding night" and does everything in his power "so that nobody except himself can have her." Yet each time he rapes her and falls asleep, "she slips out from under and cuckolds him with every man who passes by." Still, the "ifrit . . . thinks he *possesses* her" (5). This tale within a tale goes to the heart of the way male vanity depends on imagined control over the chastity of women, which in turn likely arises from a deepseated cultural anxiety about the paternity of children. Powerlessness to control the sexual activity of women, an anxiety that may have loomed larger than ever in the 1970s after William H. Masters and Virginia E. Johnson demonstrated how much more sexual, in fact, women may be than men, underlies the gynecocidal tyranny of Shahryar and the "seeming" gynecocidal tyranny of Shah Zaman. For the vengeful murders begin only after Shah Zaman surprises his beloved wife "riding astride the chief cook" and after a subsequent encounter with the famous ifrit's imprisoned girl convinces Shah Zaman and Shahryar "that no woman on earth who wants a rogering will go unrogered, though she be sealed up in a tower of brass" (43–44).

Their vengefulness may begin as a personal powerlessness to control female sexuality, probably a common anxiety. Because they are men with social power, however, their evil is magnified; their "private apocalypse" infects the state and brings on the general apocalypse (44) that finally drives Scheherazade to take action, including her own deranged plan of revenge. Here Jung's observation is again apt: "Wars, dynasties, social upheavals, conquests, and religions are but the superficial symptoms of a secret psychic attitude unknown, even to the individual himself, and transmitted by no historian." According to Jung, "the whole history of the world" ultimately springs "as a gigantic summation from . . . hidden sources in individuals."[15] Consequently, the psychosexual flaws of men like the two Shahs, who fall back on traditional models or myths of male behavior, are of paramount social significance. They may even be the ground on which the observable institutions are built.

No matter how deepseated the masculine anxiety of the two kings, their vengeful steps to gain control of feminine sexuality by destroying virgins (women with the greatest sexual potential and the greatest likelihood of chastity) do not, as the Genie/author gently points out, arise from their "real nature" (22). This gap between Shah Zaman's real na-

15. Jung, "Meaning of Psychology," 148–49.

ture and his social role, which is grandiose, compensatory, and false, explains the scheme he privately devises to sleep with the virgins sent him, thus directly addressing the sexual anxiety created by his wife's defection, but then, rather than killing them, sending them west from Samarkand to what becomes the Country of the Breastless, or the A-mazons (50–51). His plan thus saves face by protecting the part he plays socially, yet it allows him to express elements of his "real nature," an underlying love of the feminine. What he profoundly needs in order to live is "someone with whom to get on with the story of [his] life . . . a loving wife" (60). This new life he seeks from Dunyazade, but to secure it he must tell the story of his life—a truer story than any Scheherazade borrows from the Genie, one that is compelling not because he suspends it but because it comes straight from his center.

Obviously he succeeds. The ending Barth ascribes to *The Stories of the Thousand Nights and a Night* tells us as much (55). But he succeeds because he is convincing and because Dunyazade is less swallowed than Scheherazade by the compensating grandiosity of rage. This difference between the sisters may be the reason that, even though Shahryar responds to his new wife much as Shah Zaman does to the younger sister, Shahryar does "not exactly [grant] his wife the power to kill him" (53) as Shah Zaman does. The younger sister shared the older's anger at the tyranny of the brothers, but she does not allow "a fragment of personality [to detach] itself . . . and . . . harden into a shell over her mind," as a feminist novelist said of one of her characters.[16] Dunyazade remains open to the new information from Shah Zaman, and when she has reason to doubt that Scheherazade's version is the whole story, she apparently restrains herself from the irreversible action her elder sister urged her to take (38). Consequently, she is able to free herself from the world of realism ("the way it was and is") and the consequent world of moralism ("the way it ought to be") and so enter the kingdom of the imagination (the great *as if*) that Shah Zaman and Barth's postmodern fictions urge us toward, if we want to survive.

For our survival very much depends on the stories we accept or invent. As Barth's tale illustrates, for 3,500 years men (and women) have died for the story of the hero, that is, to save face. It would be, Barth shows, one of the terrible ironies one comes to expect of history

16. Ellen Glasgow, *The Sheltered Life* (Garden City, N.Y., 1932), 4.

("If a man cannot forget," Søren Kierkegaard writes in *Either/Or,* "he will never amount to much") if our own feminist revolution should liberate our culture, like Barth's Tiryns, from the myth of heroic masculinity only to have feminists themselves, like Anteia and Scheherazade, become seduced by the same myth with genders swapped. Barth, like many contemporary writers (in contrast to Eliot, Pound, and the modernists), recognizes that imitation of past models cannot create a way of life free of the mistakes of masculine heroism. Only embracing the great *as if* can lead to a culture different in the way our survival requires. *Chimera* reminds us that we must regularly go back into the treasure-house of our culture, but we must use its resources up as quickly as possible, exhaust them, in order to free the imagination from the past, which is at best only prologue to free invention, on the chance that we will discover the something new the situation requires.

Because the imagination works from the self's center, it can make effective use of the past as a resource. The past, however, as "Bellerophoniad" shows, must not be looked to for models. Instead, it is a treasure-house of mirrors, a literal funhouse. A modern writer, exhausted and blocked like the Genie/author of "Dunyazadiad" or like the author with Barth's resumé whose lecture is interjected into "Bellerophoniad" (198–203), can employ noncanonical figures such as Perseus and Bellerophon as mirrors for projections to use up the emotional possibilities of the past. In honoring the past thus, the author avoids repressing its mistakes, an error that would lead to past behaviors returning when least desired. Taking on the past in this manner, an author may be able to clean out the inner storage (earth?) closet (254) and so work through to other, less explored mirrors, such as Medusa, Melanippe, Shah Zaman, or Dunyazade. This process of exhaustion and discovery thaws possibilities otherwise frozen at the core. It reverses the energy exchange that modernism fostered through symbolic mimesis. Rather than have modern characters, Wastelanders, Leopold Blooms, Joe Christmases, unwittingly imitate patterns passed down, Barth's approach addresses the archetypes directly, frames them, uses them up, and moves to less explored mythic and psychological territory.

Barth illustrates this process by contrasting the Genie/author in "Dunyazadiad" with the ambitious author Jerome B. Bray in "Bellerophoniad" (246–57). Bray's problem is that of Bellerophon, if Bellerophon were a writer rather than a Greek hero. Caught up in American bicentennial fever, Bray dreams grandiosely of creating a Revolutionary Novel (249) and plans to do so by combining external patterns and following various formulae for fictions (250–52).[17] Bray's approach incorporates whatever it comes across, including materials from the author of *Giles Goat-Boy* (248–50), but adds little of himself to them. He ends up in litigation, paranoid, frustrated, and unfunded (257).

Bray's imitative pursuit of novelty differs significantly from the approach employed by the Genie/author, whose non-Persian name, to judge by Dunyazade's description of him (8), must be "John Barth." The Genie works, like the blocked modern author in "Bellerophoniad" (211), as his inner energy moves him. Since his university days, he has followed his passion for Scheherazade (12). She is not only a mirror image of his young new mistress but also the model for him of the storyteller's position (inasmuch as she must publish, that is, tell a good story, or perish) and thus his muse (16). Most important, his focus on her, his affection for her, enables him when he is blocked to "go back to the original springs of narrative" (10) in order to go beyond his past works.

Yet the Genie-as-Barth frames and thus undercuts Scheherazade's story three times: with Dunyazade's, Shah Zaman's, as well as his own tale, in which he supplies the great storyteller the stories for which she is remembered (13). In the end of "Dunyazadiad," the wistful third part that is the true ending of *Chimera,* he has worked through his dependence on the elder sister as a model and settled on Dunyazade and Shah Zaman as mirrors of the great *as if* in himself, the set of

17. At the same time, Bray is an American parody of a French New Novelist. Alain Robbe-Grillet had hoped to keep the novel always new by extending the tradition of modernism, especially as found in Marcel Proust, Faulkner, and Samuel Beckett, and combining that tradition with the ontology of the phenomenologists. This ambition led him to declare in 1957 that traditional views of character, story, commitment, form, and content were "obsolete notions." In his own novel revolution, Jerome Bray makes a similar proclamation: "On the one hand, inasmuch as 'character,' 'plot,' and for that matter 'content,' 'subject,' and 'meaning,' are attributes of particular novels, the Revolutionary Novel *NOTES* is to dispense with all of them in order to transcend the limitations of particularity; . . . it will represent nothing beyond itself, have no content except its own form, no subject but its own processes" (256). Ultimately, however, despite the wish to transcend the elements of past fictions, Bray's Revolutionary Novel, determined as it would be by computers, numbers, and past patterns, seems very different from Robbe-Grillet's vision of a novel that would enable its reader "to learn to invent his own life." See Robbe-Grillet, *For a New Novel,* 25–47, 140–41, 156.

possibilities represented by the young couple who greet "sister and brother in the forenoon of a new life" in which the "second half . . . will be sweeter than the first" (55–56), even though the Great Destroyer awaits them all. The Genie's center has been constant, but at its new depth it has a new look and a new name, Dunyazade rather than Scheherazade. He has exhausted the energy Scheherazade once held for him in order to reach resources mirrored by her little sister.

When we seek to tie the Genie's emotional development and parallel processes represented in *Chimera* to established psychological models, we discover that Barth's mix is complex and that the patterns rejected are easier to identify than the processes treated most favorably. On the one hand, as indicated in the earlier discussion of "Life-Story," Protean figures such as Polyeidus are familiar embodiments in contemporary fiction of the phenomenological type derived from positions the philosophical heirs of Husserl, especially Sartre, have taken. On the other hand, characters who wed themselves to a fixed role grounded in a seemingly fixed destiny and do so in order to compensate for a sense of inferiority, especially Perseus with his organ inferiority, appear at first glance to follow Alfred Adler's familiar notion that greatness grows from the need to make up for a perceived flaw.[18] Adler's view of such compensation is far less negative than Barth's, for Barth directs much of his slashing satire at those who, like Bellerophon/Deliades, Shahryar, and the oft-rejected Anteia, try to disguise damaged self-esteem with the grandiose masculine posturing the myth of the hero sanctions.

We find stronger parallels if we compare Barth's compensators to models of narcissistic grandiosity and rage described by Heinz Kohut.[19] Although Kohut's major essays and books are contemporaneous with Barth's and therefore not probable influences, both authors are likely reacting to similar excesses in a culture often identified as more narcissistic than past ages or perhaps to similar literary characters, including Melville's rageful Captain Ahab. Whatever the explanation, it helps us understand the way the myth of the hero functions in *Chimera* if we accept Kohut's suggestion that the grandiose false

18. Lifton, *Boundaries,* 45–49; Alfred Adler, *The Science of Living,* ed. Heinz L. Ansbacher (Garden City, N.Y., 1969), 1–2; Alfred Adler, *The Individual Psychology of Alfred Adler,* ed. Heinz L. Ansbacher and Rowena R. Ansbacher (New York, 1956), 360.

19. Kohut, *Self Psychology,* 135–36, 141–60.

self covers over, and thereby represses, the low self-esteem that results from inner hollowness, from the lack of the solid center Kohut calls the "nuclear self." From his perspective, the Protean quality that phenomenology espouses, far from being a functional pattern "necessary to life in our times," would be reinterpreted as an indication of the fragmentation of the self that he finds portrayed in twentieth century arts from the great modernists onward.[20] Indeed, as Barth represents it, the Proteanism of Polyeidus has got so out of his control (152, 206–207) that it is dysfunctional, if not bordering on the pathological, as was that of the "Life-Story" narrator.

In contrast, the characters in *Chimera* who attract the reader's emotions live, as we have seen, from a stable center, a nucleus of needs and ambitions that avoids the fragmentation of Proteanism. Their center, however, never demands the rigidity typical of characters who are driven by a fixed identity and destiny. Medusa's actions toward Perseus, for example, are positive from first to last, even though her emotions have to remain open enough to accept the fact that he is both her deliverer and her beheader. Or again: Melanippe manages her culturally mandated Amazon role yet cherishes her private identity. Shah Zaman similarly supports his public role as patriarchal ruler while living from a core that assists the women he "officially" has raped and murdered. Dunyazade and the Genie likewise possess sufficient flexibility to shift focus, she from Scheherazade to Shah Zaman, he from Scheherazade to Dunyazade, without losing control of their capacity to change or losing contact with nuclear ideals and ambitions.

The nature of this center that certain of Barth's characters possess and others lack is difficult to describe. When Perseus reminds Medusa that in their mortal days they "were archetypes, not stereo types; reality, not myth" (129), Barth (if not Perseus) is clearly playing on a central element of the Jungian model of individuation, a process that underlies Joseph Campbell's heroic monomyth so often employed by Barth (261).[21] This allusion to Jung may indicate that the center of the self consists of energies represented by the archetypal figures, includ-

20. Heinz Kohut and Ernest S. Wolf, "The Disorders of the Self and Their Treatment: An Outline," *International Journal of Psycho-Analysis,* LIX (1978), 416–17, 419, 421; Lifton, *Boundaries,* 44; Kohut and Wolf, "Disorders of the Self," 417–18; Kohut, *Self Psychology,* 193, 245.

21. Joseph Campbell, *The Hero with a Thousand Faces* (Princeton, 1972), 17–18, 245.

ing the hero, the temptress, the various gods and goddesses, and so forth. Yet when Barth's double in "Bellerophoniad" proposes, in contrast to the modernists, to take the right "end of the mythopoeic stick" and "address the archetypes directly" (199), he clearly intends to get beyond the archetypes, which, unexamined, are oftentimes (even in the great modernist works) given dominion over individual lives and cultures, thereby turning out Bellerophon-like imitations of the archetypal patterns.

A way out of this psychological quagmire may exist. Clearly Barth is warning us that the archetypal life lived slavishly becomes a stereotypic evasion of life, an abstract ideal held in the mind. In his resistance to abstraction, he stands solidly in the mainstream of his southern literary heritage. At the same time, however, by pointing us toward the original energies of Perseus and the less familiar energies of Medusa, Melanippe, Dunyazade, and his Genie-self, he is reminding us that the archetypes, even for Jung, are not the seemingly universal figures and images of myths, legends, religions, and folklore—not the symbols—but the human *energies,* the elemental instincts and behaviors, that those images express.[22] Only our less familiar, noncanonical myths, or newly invented ones, can set the central energies of the human spirit, the psyche, free from the patterns into which the canonical myths we take for reality have channeled the inward resources. Read in proper order, the tales of *Chimera* record the process whereby their author exhausted the familiar heroic myth in order to release the energies of other myths waiting at the periphery of Western consciousness.

22. Charles B. Harris, *Passionate Virtuosity: The Fiction of John Barth* (Urbana, 1983), 130–55, esp. 143.

VI The New Philosopher's Stone: Lawrence Durrell's *The Avignon Quintet*

In *Sebastian,* the fourth novel of *The Avignon Quintet,* Lawrence Durrell equates the Protean pattern with pathology when his narrator judges the homicidal maniac Mnemidis thus: "[The] mad must be people without selves: their whole investment is in the other, the object. They are ruled by the forces of total uncertainty."[1] Although this statement seems a clear attack on Sartre's phenomenological position that the "I" is "consciousness of objects," Durrell is no exponent of the unitary or discrete personality. Since *Justine,* which appeared in 1957, his novels have dealt expertly with the multiple adumbrations of a single character. But no matter how Protean his major figures become, their diversity, like the diversity of Pynchon's Fausto Maijstral, contains an underlying unity that Durrell calls the dominant or proclivity or predilection of the personality. The quest for Durrell then is to permit his characters to entertain a diversity likely beyond Fausto's dreams yet not to lose the dominant note of their personality. In this quest, as in the quest of the famed alchemists, the philosopher's stone is the key to success. In the *Quintet,* his inadequately reviewed new series of novels, the stone takes on an especially modern form.[2]

1. Lawrence Durrell, *Sebastian, or Ruling Passions* (New York, 1984), 160.

2. Robert F. Moss, in "*Monsieur* by Lawrence Durrell," *New Republic,* February 22, 1975, p. 30, for example, speaks of the author's "crippled genius," and D. J. Enright, in "Great Slow Verbs," *Listener,* October 17, 1974, p. 513, finds *Monsieur* pretentious, banal,

Early in the *Quintet,* Quatrefages tells the central character, Aubrey Blanford, that the fabled treasure of the Templars for which Lord Galen and eventually Hitler's emissaries search is only a decoy or symbol for something far more important: "What does it *matter* if there is a treasure or not? . . . I think there is no treasure; I think Philippe Le Bel got it all. I have not mentioned this to anyone because I am not absolutely sure—but our search for the quincunx of trees concerns another sort of treasure. That is what I really believe" (*LV,* 163). At the end of *The Avignon Quintet,* just when the narrative has carried us through the first cave of the cavern where the treasure ought to have been hidden and we as readers are prepared to advance in procession with the characters "down the inner corridors" to the solution to the centuries-old mystery, Blanford uses the last sentence left in the series to think "that if ever he wrote the scene he would say: 'It was at this precise moment that reality prime rushed to the aid of fiction and the totally unpredictable began to take place!' "[3] Barring the transformation of the quintet into a sextet, readers must come to terms with Quatrefages' comment that, for us at least, there is no Templar's treasure, or if there is, it is "another sort of treasure." But what sort? That is my concern here, and to answer this question, which may be the central mystery of the series, we will find it helpful to rise above Durrell's "quincunx of trees" to comprehend the pattern of the forest itself. Among other things, Durrell in *The Avignon Quintet* has attempted to capture, as though in a mirror, the movements of Aubrey Blanford's spirit as it prepares for the act of creation. Durrell establishes the nature of this movement (represented, we shall see, by the philosopher's stone) in the first and second volumes, *Monsieur,* published in 1974, and *Livia,* in 1978, which constitute the specific interests of this essay.

That Quatrefages should deny the treasure's existence may unsettle the reader, for Quatrefages has organized Lord Galen's quest, and the quest, a recurring motif of the series, generates much of the suspense

---

shabby, and trivial. Similar objections to the first two novels of the series appear in reviews by John Skow, Anthony Thwaite, and Julian Barnes, among others. James P. Carley, in "Lawrence Durrell's Avignon Quincunx and Gnostic Heresy," *Malahat Review,* LXI (1982), 156–67, was first to give the early books the attention they deserve, but without the perspective that the later ones, especially *Quinx,* provide.

3. Lawrence Durrell, *Quinx, or The Ripper's Tale* (New York, 1986), 201.

in the final three volumes, *Constance, Sebastian,* and *Quinx,* which came out in 1982, 1983, and 1985, respectively. As with the mysteries surrounding the Templar's Gnosticism and the related cult of suicide and euthanasia, however, Durrell simply refuses to respond to the reader's desire for either a literal solution or a resolved outward action. These refusals, I imagine, explain more than anything else does why the *Quintet* has not created the literary sensation that greeted *The Alexandria Quartet* in the sixties. Certainly the *Quintet* does not want for excellent writing: the first, second, fourth, and fifth volumes are tight and pregnant with meaning; and even though *Constance* is more loosely constructed, it (like *Mountolive* before it) is jammed with enough drama between clearly defined characters to generate the excitement of popular fiction, provided the reader has mastered Durrell's purpose in *Monsieur* and *Livia* well enough to feel comfortable with the characters. To understand his purpose, though, we must first come to terms with what Blanford calls "the Philosopher's Stone."

When he hears Quatrefages' doubts, Blanford says he understands a little bit about Quatrefages' other sort of treasure: "You mean the Philosopher's Stone, don't you?" (*LV,* 163). Blanford thus creates an equation between treasure, or gold, and philosopher's stone that Durrell had earlier made in his 1963 play, *An Irish Faustus,* where the title character receives, at the death of his old master, Tremethius, a ring said to be "made / Of alchemist's gold—the true stone!"[4] Traditionally, the philosopher's stone was the goal of the alchemists' grand quest: whether reckoned an actual stone or another substance, it was believed to have the power of transmuting baser metals into gold. But this power is probably not what Blanford means. Certainly it, in the literal sense, is not what Durrell gives the reader in the five novels.

In *Monsieur,* the Gnostic banker Akkad asserts that the stone is "the Holy Grail of the ancient consciousness" (*Mr,* 222). Similarly, in our century the philosopher's stone of alchemy has come to represent "the 'conjunction' of opposites, or the integration of the conscious self with the feminine or unconscious side"; it stands as "a symbol of the All." This psychic meaning emerges from the elaborate alchemical studies of Jung, who stressed the esoteric dimension of alchemy. He noted particularly that though many alchemists seemed to search for a me-

4. Lawrence Durrell, *An Irish Faustus: A Morality in Nine Scenes* (New York, 1964), 27. Ian S. MacNiven brought this connection to my attention.

chanical means of transmuting baser metals to gold, the true initiates sought an uncommon gold (*aurum non vulgi*), or "philosophical gold" (*aurum philosophicum*), a goal that he and other Jungian thinkers take to have represented spiritual values and psychic transformation.[5]

Jung himself stressed the manner in which the special conjunction represented by the stone corresponded to the transference that he and Freud agreed to be the "main problem of medical psychotherapy." Loosely defined, the transference, as he writes, is the "relationship between doctor and patient . . . a more or less unconscious identification of doctor and patient." For the Freudians, the unassimilated feelings of transferences revolve specifically around the parents and siblings as experienced in early childhood. The Jungians broaden the concept. In the language of Ann Belford Ulanov, the transference "occurs when one person becomes the carrier for [any] unconscious content activated in another person," which then "carries into the present moment conflicting and unassimilated feelings about figures in the past that distort the perception of the present person or situation."[6] For Ulanov, the transference is thus a special form of unconscious projection. In Durrell's *Quintet* it is this expanded process of transference, or projection, that constitutes the philosopher's stone for Aubrey Blanford.

In *Livia,* the characters interested in the Templars' treasure all have competing notions of what the treasure might be. Lord Galen, an international banker preoccupied with the delicious anal gnawing of money (*LV,* 13, 81, 240), sponsors the search from a motive similar to the motive of literal alchemy, the desire for gold. But his clerk and statistician, Quatrefages, who actually conducts Galen's search "in the tangled mass of documentation which surrounds the Templars and their heresy," does not deny Blanford's intuition that Quatrefages is seeking the elusive philosopher's stone. As a defrocked curate filled with atheistic despair (*LV,* 90), Quatrefages may at some unconscious level take the stone the way Jung later did, as a natural parallel to Christ.[7]

5. J. E. Cirlot, *A Dictionary of Symbols* (New York, 1962), 300; Jung, *Memories, Dreams, Reflections,* 210 n. 11.

6. Jung, *Memories, Dreams, Reflections,* 137, 212; Ulanov, "Transference/Countertransference," 68.

7. Jung, *Memories, Dreams, Reflections,* 210.

The character of central concern here and throughout the series, though, is Aubrey Blanford, and his interest in the philosopher's stone, whatever he may take it to mean in his original conversation with Quatrefages, becomes, as his literary and psychological career in the series shows, a profound demonstration of what the stone as transference, or conjunction, can mean to modern man and postmodern fiction. As we read *Livia,* we quickly sense that *Monsieur* is the product of Blanford's own repeated and complex projections on friends he knew during the part of his youth spent in Avignon. Indeed, the relationship of the second novel in the series to the first resembles that of a literary biography, or disguised autobiography (*Livia*), to a novel (*Monsieur*) written by Blanford, who is the subject of the biography. In this case, however, both the "novel" and the "biography" are fictions written by the same author, Durrell, who "begat / Blanford (who begat Tu and Sam and Livia) / who begat / Sutcliffe" and so on, as the "Envoi" to *Monsieur* indicates (*Mr,* 311).

It is, I suggest, Blanford's organic process of projection that structures the *Quintet.* The process recapitulates phases similar to those of Jungian individuation, the pattern of psychological development by which one integrates the dark side and the contrasexual energies of the personality with consciousness. Once we grasp the *Quintet* in its entirety, this pattern turns what Blanford calls a teratoma, "a bag full of unfinished spare parts—nails and hair and half-grown teeth" (*LV,* 17), into a unified series of novels organized somewhat like the crowning work of Khmer architecture, Angkor Wat, Cambodia. Blanford's novelist and double, Rob Sutcliffe, in one of his notebooks describes Angkor Wat as "five-coned towers" that "form a quincunx" (*Mr,* 267); the great temple mountain in fact consists of four corner shrines plus a taller one that stands in the square's middle and indicates the hub of the universe. This is the configuration toward which Durrell aspires in the new series, with *Monsieur,* perhaps, standing at the center and providing "a cluster of themes to be reworked in the others" (*LV,* 11). The central action of the series, then, is not the outward search for the treasure but the inward process by which Aubrey Blanford uses his fictive imagination to recover the lost and ignored dimensions of himself.

As early as 1960 in a letter to Richard Aldington, Durrell revealed his interest in Jung's view of the philosopher's stone. Discussing the role of the homunculi in *Clea,* he wrote: "I bet you have seen Jung's work on alchemy and psychoanalysis in which the search for the Philosopher's stone is studied . . . and so on. I'm trying to use these things like crude symbolisms." Earlier still, in a November, 1936, letter to Henry Miller, he indicated that he already understood the essence of what the philosopher's stone as projection could mean to literature; there he calls *Hamlet* "a perfect picture of the inner struggle, done in terms of the outer one—as all great books are, at least to me" and "a marvellous picture of psychic and social disorganisation in an individual." Apparently Jung's alchemical studies provided Durrell with the stone to stand as a succinct symbol, a convenient mytheme charged with positive associations, for a process that he already recognized in Shakespeare's play and other great books. In the *Quintet,* then, he has chosen to treat explicitly what he and others take to be a mainstay of the imagination implicit in fictions since Homer: the need to turn characters inside out in order to reveal the inner struggle in terms of the outer.[8]

In parallel fashion the modern attention in psychology to transference and projection simply foregrounds a process that has always colored personal relationships. For Jungians, all the unconscious contents we must experience in order to develop psychologically are "first recognized and reacted to" when we project unconscious qualities of our own onto outer objects. Indeed, projections so govern one's behavior that in the Gestalt therapy of Frederick S. Perls the concept of projection is expanded to explain dreams; for Perls, the dream is a projection of the self: "That is, all of the dream components, large or small, human or non-human, are representations of the dreamer."[9] In the two volumes that open the *Quintet,* Durrell goes as far with Perls as making the primary characters other than Blanford, all the figures in the seemingly outward action, either the projections of Blanford's waking

8. Ian S. MacNiven and Harry T. Moore, eds., *Literary Lifelines: The Richard Aldington—Lawrence Durrell Correspondence* (New York, 1981), 179, ellipsis in letter as published; George Wickes, ed., *Lawrence Durrell and Henry Miller: A Private Correspondence* (New York, 1963), 26; E. R. Dodds, *The Greeks and the Irrational* (Berkeley, 1968), 14–17.

9. Ulanov, "Transference/Countertransference," 68–69; Edinger, "Outline of Analytical Psychology," 4; Erving Polster and Miriam Polster, *Gestalt Therapy Integrated: Contours of Theory and Practice* (New York, 1973), 265; Frederick Perls, Ralph E. Hefferline, and Paul Goodman, *Gestalt Therapy: Excitement and Growth in the Human Personality* (New York, 1951), 221.

dream or screens for his projections. In this way the other characters, by presenting the otherwise unconscious elements of Blanford's psychic life to his conscious mind, mirror the separate stages of his search for the philosopher's stone of modern life.

A basic strategy of *Monsieur* and *Livia* then is to underscore the manifold ways in which Blanford transfers his own unconscious needs and fears onto his friends (Sam, Hilary, Constance, Livia, Lord Galen, Felix Chatto, Quatrefages, and lesser acquaintances) as he invents the imaginary beings of *Monsieur:* Piers de Nogaret, Sylvie, Bruce Drexel, Rob Sutcliffe, Lord Banquo, and the others through whom he inaugurates his quest for psychic integration. Like the other novels in the new series, the first pair therefore are largely about the varied interrelationships of life and art revolving around the projection process that Blanford discovers and employs during the phases of his life covered by the series. Viewed thus, the *Quintet* is the *Künstlerroman* of Aubrey Blanford, much the way the *Quartet* is Darley's. But here, by thematizing the actual projection process and examining it directly, Durrell has created a series even more challenging than Darley's stories, which used the various supporting characters, Melissa, Justine, Leila, Clea, or Arnauti, Balthazar, Mountolive, Pursewarden, and so forth, in the traditional literary way: to tell Darley's inner story in terms of the outer story of his friends taken as real characters.

In the new series, Rob Sutcliffe, for example, seems more difficult to grasp than does Pursewarden or Arnauti because Durrell continually reminds us that Rob, who frequently seems more real than Arnauti ever did, is a being of a radically different imaginary status than the real characters in the *Quartet.* Blanford openly invents Sutcliffe as a totally imaginary alternate self, a once-famous novelist who, wounded by his wife's defection with another woman, becomes a charlatan (*Mr,* 12, 185, 239). Sutcliffe is thus a fictional mirror of the cynical, skeptical, self-critical, yet earthy side of Blanford himself.

In addition, in *Livia,* Durrell takes us into Blanford's workshop so that we may follow Sutcliffe's life from his birth in one of Blanford's schoolboy diaries (*LV,* 115) through a richer childhood (*LV,* 24) and into an earthier young manhood than his creator ever knew (*LV,* 55–61). In time the imaginary creature is almost as real to Blanford as Blanford is to himself (*LV,* 1). For example, when Blanford wants to use Sutcliffe as a distancing device and treats him as the author of his own series of novels that begins with *Monsieur* (*LV,* 11), Sutcliffe, thinking he has the power to assign his own titles to Blanford's books, renames the novel *The Prince of Darkness.* After Blanford feels compelled to kill Sutcliffe at the end of *Monsieur*—"it was literally him or me," for "we couldn't both commit suicide" (*Mr,* 297)—Rob still has enough hold of Blanford's imagination in *Livia* to tell his inventor to bring him back from the dead (*LV,* 6). Blanford obeys, so that Sutcliffe can author "a quincunx of novels set out in a good classical order" that will "demonstrate how Livia [Blanford's own defecting wife] was tailored down to the sad size of Pia," Sutcliffe's wife in *Monsieur* (*LV,* 11). In time, Rob threatens to turn the tables on Blanford: "What would you give me if I wrote a book to prove that the great Blanford is simply the fiction of one of his fictions?" (*LV,* 53). In fact, in *Monsieur* Sutcliffe himself has invented a novelist named "Bloshford," whom Sutcliffe detests for his bestsellers, his two Rolls-Royces, and his Venetian life (*Mr,* 183). The struggles between Blanford and Sutcliffe provide some of the brightest self-reflexive fireworks in this consummate group of postmodern novels.

The further complexity of Blanford's projections shows up in that Blanford's dark double, Sutcliffe, has his own double, Toby Goddard, the historian of the Knights Templar and of their heresy (*Mr,* 76). Sutcliffe and Toby are so alike that Bruce Drexel, the narrator of much of *Monsieur,* calls them "Gog and Magog, two huge shortsighted men with sandy unruly hair and colourless eyelashes; specialists in laughter and irremediable *gaffes.*" When he was "looking down at the sleeping Toby [Drexel] was also seeing Rob Sutcliffe" (*Mr,* 76). The reference to Gog and Magog, the two wicker-and-plaster giants once carried in the procession of the lord mayor of London, takes the reader back to the origin of Rob and Toby in a common source; for each character is an imaginary part of Blanford, much as Gog and Magog were halves of Gogmagog, the twelve-foot giant who occupied Britain before the coming of Brutus, the legendary founder of the British race. The Gog and Magog comparisons for Sutcliffe and Toby underscore the process of psychological division repeated throughout the *Quintet,* a technique that combines projections with the companion tendency of subdividing the personality through doubling and splitting off aspects of the self.[10] Such projections, which, Durrell implies, could theoretically

10. Lawrence Durrell, *Constance, or Solitary Practices* (New York, 1982), 1.

be repeated to infinity, reproduce and at the same time distance elements of the self.

In *Monsieur,* Blanford further divides himself to create Bruce Drexel, the medical attaché at the British Embassy in Paris (*Mr,* 4), who serves as chief narrator and putative author of the early parts of the novel. Although we learn in *Livia* that Blanford once had a doctor called Bruce in Paris (*LV,* 204), the opening paragraphs of *Monsieur* indicate that Bruce is actually another double of Blanford: "How well I remembered, how well he [Bruce] remembered! The Bruce that I was, and the Bruce I become as I jot down these words, a few every day" (*Mr,* 3).

That the "I" here may also refer to Sutcliffe becomes clear later in the book when Bruce discovers among the dead Sutcliffe's papers evidence that Sutcliffe had been writing a novel that began with the exact words that open *Monsieur,* though his hero was to have been called "something like Oakshot" (*Mr,* 192–93). Because Bruce may also be a mask of Sutcliffe, we infer, as we read *Monsieur,* that the inversion haunting the sexual triangle of Bruce, his wife Sylvie, and her brother Piers de Nogaret was invented as a fictional mirror of the inversion that torments Sutcliffe in his three-cornered marriage to Pia, especially after she runs off with Trash, the black woman she really loves. The implication is that Pia married Sutcliffe to cover her lesbian attachment much the way Bruce married Sylvie to mask his loving Piers (*Mr,* 18). In *Livia,* however, we learn that the two "case histories" in *Monsieur* (*LV,* 238), the one regarding Bruce's confusion over Piers and Sylvie and the other Sutcliffe's hurt by Pia, are Blanford's efforts to work out in fiction both his own confusion for loving Constance (Tu) and perhaps her brother Hilary yet marrying their sister Livia (*LV,* 12) as well as his bitterness about Livia's defection with Thrush, her dark lover from Martinique (*LV,* 67–68).

With these parallels in mind, we begin to understand the purpose of Blanford's projections. What is most obvious, they provide defenses; they permit him to distance himself from his most conflicted emotions: his ambivalence and his narcissistic wounds. For in the larger part of *Monsieur* it is not Blanford's wife who abandons her husband; it is Sutcliffe's. Nor is it Blanford's ambivalence over brothers and sisters; it is Bruce's. Wearing the double masks of Sutcliffe and Bruce, Blanford feels freer to deal with the most powerful and difficult emotional events in his life.

Yet Blanford ultimately does not deny that these painful episodes belong to him. If ever in his life he repressed these private materials (say, before writing *Monsieur*), the creation of the fictional characters puts his psychic turmoil before him once again and in a more objective form that allows him to reexperience his traumas and better come to terms with them; through his writing he will fully become what his traumas have made him and so, in a salutary way, forget them (*Mr,* 7). His fictional characters are true transference phenomena; or, in the language of Freudian revisionist Heinz Kohut, they are true selfobjects: aspects of Blanford's environment that "at the same time are part of [Blanford's] self."[11] In *Livia,* we begin to pick up enough clues to Blanford's damaging first years with a distant father and intrusive mother (*LV,* 21–25) to appreciate the childhood facts that go into his creating selfobjects out of Constance, Livia, and other friends, both real and invented. Moreover, the open treatment of Livia as Livia in the novel bearing her name rather than as Pia indicates that Blanford is directly reclaiming (by re-collecting or introjecting) the painful materials first projected on the fictional characters in *Monsieur.* Through his fictional creations the conflicts bottled up or masked in his unconscious find a way to return to consciousness. This new self-understanding constitutes the uncommon gold that the philosopher's stone of Blanford's fictions transmutes out of the dark dross of his psychological conflict.

Although Blanford's journey toward self-integration is not complete in *Livia,* the pastoral tone of the second novel relative to the Gothic atmosphere in *Monsieur* indicates the direction of his psychological movement. His characters do not yet "dance" the way Darley's do at the end of the *Quartet,* nor are they yet in spirited procession the way they will be at the end of *Quinx.* Nevertheless, the contrast between the world of Piers's Verfeuille (after the Macabru experience) and the world of Constance's Tu Duc seems very much one between age and youth, night and day, and reveals both the nature of Blanford's growth and his ability to acknowledge all sides of his being, including the dark and the light. In the second novel he has already begun to benefit from his fictional approach to life.

Framed by *Livia,* the desperate Gnosticism of *Monsieur* takes on a

11. Wolf, "Psychoanalytic Psychology," 43–44.

new significance, one more psychological and less theological and philosophical than it possesses in the first novel read in isolation.[12] For Piers's willingness to embrace the dark view of life expressed by Gnosticism seems appropriate for minds wrecked by the repeated confusions that have beset him and his creator.

Every important relationship in Piers's life is shot through with ambivalence. As a French diplomat committed to overseeing his nation's foreign affairs, he considers himself the last of the cosmopolitan Knights Templar (*Mr,* 25). Yet he knows that his own Templar heritage resembles the relationship of Judas to Christianity, for his famous ancestor had penetrated the order as the secret agent of the French king Philippe Le Bel, who used the intelligence thus collected to destroy the order. His ancestor's motives were simply to avenge his own grandparents, according to Piers himself (*Mr,* 170), or his parents, according to Toby Goddard's history (*Mr,* 247), Cathars and thus heretics who, according to legend, were burnt at the stake by the order (*Mr,* 170). As a reward for the betrayal, the de Nogaret family received its rich lands, manors, rivers, farms, and the old chateau of Verfeuille (*Mr,* 171). Already the self-acknowledged "descendant of Judas" (*Mr,* 171), Piers compounds his guilt by abandoning his family estate and failing in ignorance to save it from financial disaster (*Mr,* 45, 55).

In addition, Piers bears the burden of the relationship he, Bruce, and Sylvie share. Far heavier on him than his inverted affection for Bruce weighs what the two of them have done to Sylvie. She stands at the center of the three-headed single self they have become (*Mr,* 8, 220), much like the narrator Bruce-Sutcliffe-Blanford. Not only did she love them both enough to marry Bruce and so cement the triangle (*Mr,* 7–8), but none of them was able to say who fathered the child she deliberately miscarried (*Mr,* 18). With no distance at all between her childhood and adult lovers, she has drowned in "meaning" (*Mr,* 23), so that even numbers seem eroticized in her madness (*Mr,* 26), and thus spends her years in the mental asylum, Montfavet at Avignon, talking to her dead brother (*Mr,* 6), going over his papers (*Mr,* 21–22), and blaming herself for having given him too much sleeping potion (*Mr,* 28). Even before Piers's apparent suicide (the event that calls

12. This is the manner in which Carley, "Durrell's Avignon Quincunx," discusses the Gnosticism in *Monsieur,* as though it were not framed by *Livia.*

Bruce back to Avignon and so starts *Monsieur*), Piers has charged himself with having killed his sister (*Mr,* 25), though she survives him. To his tortured psyche, the Gnostic vision of the Egyptian banker Akkad comes as the first and most satisfying balm to his deep thirst to believe (*Mr,* 94, 106, 164). For Gnosticism speaks of a universe created by a true god who has died, a universe now governed through the Great Lie and usurped by the Prince of Darkness (*Mr,* 113, 118, 119), a universe devoted to gold, excrement, usury, and material greed (*Mr,* 141–42).

Even in *Monsieur,* however, Piers's dark vision stands balanced in Blanford's imagination by the perspectives that Bruce Drexel and Rob Sutcliffe provide. Bruce persists in considering much of Gnosticism nonsense (*Mr,* 9, 124), and Sutcliffe, who thinks right sex "a capital endeavor" (*Mr,* 205), calls Akkad's dark god an abortion (*Mr,* 220) and goes on to create the fictional Oakshot, who condemns both Gnostic suicide and Cathar abstinence from sex (*Mr,* 200). Even so, the dominance of Gnosticism here clearly makes this first novel Blanford's Book of the Shadow, that is, in Jungian parlance, the dark, repressed side of the personal self. *Monsieur* brings back into consciousness the various ambivalences, disappointments, and guilts Blanford shares with Bruce, Piers, and Sutcliffe, plus deep rages his fictional friends do not, in the first novel, experience: anger at the mindless destructions of World War II, specifically the Nazi occupation of France, and at the (for Blanford) debilitating deaths of the friends of his youth and his imagination, especially the "defections" of Tu (*Mr,* 305) and Sutcliffe (*Mr,* 5, 13). However dark, this guilt and anger nonetheless belong to the fund of materials with which Blanford the novelist must work. The philosopher's stone of projection has refunded these emotions from the troublesome caves of the unconscious to well-lighted chambers where they now participate in the dance of the five novels.

The title of the second volume, *Livia,* suggests that in a Jungian pattern of individual development or individuation, this book should be the Book of the Anima, the feminine projection of Blanford. And it is, but largely of the negative anima, the seductive and destructive feminine component that Blanford in his young manhood projected on the woman he married. Livia is the dark member (*LV,* 5) of three siblings (with blond Constance, or Tu, and even blonder Hilary) and, in a psychological sense, is a girl fashioned out of a boy, more a male *quaire* than a female (*LV,* 8). Yet when Aubrey Blanford is young and fresh out of Oxford, she seems the sexual trigger his blood requires (*LV,* 9–10). These truths about Livia are so painful for Aubrey that even after he has invented Pia largely in Livia's image, he still must call on Sutcliffe to express them for him. The manifest plot of *Livia* follows Aubrey through his painful relationship with her. It recollects how Livia schemed to break up the budding love of Aubrey and Constance; for she so loved her sister that she could not bear the complicity of Constance and Aubrey (*LV,* 38–39, 42). It recounts Aubrey's reactions both when he sees Livia naked with the woman he set to spy on her (*LV,* 13) and after he learns of the various female lovers she has had before and since their marriage (*LV,* 16, 105, 141, 153). It traces her inversion to her desire for a mock incest that would join her to the mother who wounded her by vanishing abroad (*LV,* 42–43, 66–67). It follows Livia through her career as a young Cubist painter in Paris (*LV,* 66), her attraction to Germany in the 1920s (*LV,* 108), her growing anti-Lenin and anti-Jewish sentiments (*LV,* 109), her turn to Aryan propaganda (*LV,* 109), and her eventual participation in a Bavarian rally, where she is seen wearing a German uniform (*LV,* 179). Livia, thus, is as much the dark side of the Europe of her generation as she is the negative feminine energy of Blanford.

As Durrell balanced the Gnostic darkness of *Monsieur* with the doubts of Bruce and Sutcliffe, so in *Livia* he embeds the destructive behavior of the title figure in a matrix of opposite forces, represented especially by Constance and the tumbledown mansion the sisters inherit, Tu Duc, set in a land of amazing "beauty and richness" (*LV,* 9, 49, 51). Although the movement of the novel proves to be the increasingly irresistible drift toward World War II, a momentum that by itself supports the Gnostic axiom that this world belongs to Monsieur, the pastoral life Constance offers her young friends at Tu Duc quietly demonstrates that the Gnostic principle, if not an illusion, is a partial truth at best. The novel ends with a massive *pompe à merde* that Blanford thinks is "sucking out the intellectual excrement of the twentieth century in a town which was once Rome" (*LV,* 262). Whereas this work is done only at night, in the daytime Avignon sits in a "green and innocent country" (*LV,* 263). Similarly, at the end, when Hassad the Egyptian prince throws his *Satyricon*-like banquet, complete with women *bien en chair* hired from Marseille and Toulouse (*LV,* 251), Constance, Blanford, and their friends witness the grand spectacle from the stable vantage point of the Pont du Gard, surrounded by a "dark lambent sky" and "a dense dew . . . ripe with the premonitions of the harvest" (*LV,* 260).

In many ways, Constance herself embodies the positive qualities of her house and region. In contrast to her sister, she is "made for deep attachments as a cello is made for music" (*LV,* 9). Both a friend and a disciple of Freud, whom she considers the greatest thinker in Europe (*LV,* 178), she possesses not only sufficient perception to explain Livia to Blanford (*LV,* 15) but the added self-understanding to overcome in her own psyche the mother-hatred that dominates her sister's life (*LV,* 44, 65). Although after her husband Sam dies she has no wish to remarry, she nonetheless carries on a long love affair with Blanford (*LV,* 21), who loved her even before he fell for Livia (*LV,* 12). In the way that Livia brought to consciousness the negative drives of the woman buried inside Blanford, Constance herself gives every indication of carrying Blanford's positive feminine projections. Each woman is part of the philosopher's stone of self-recognition that once enabled Blanford to become the fully creative man (*LV,* 20, 154–55, 164). It is apparently as much to bring the dead Tu back to life (*LV,* 4–6) as the dead Sutcliffe (*LV,* 6) and the missing Livia back to him (*LV,* 20) that Blanford continues in old age to seek the "consolations of art against the central horrors of death" (*LV,* 5). Although finally chimerical, the consolations of his endeavor contain substantial psychic rewards.

No matter how completely the world may seem to belong to the Gnostic Prince, Constance re-collected reminds Blanford of what she alive once told him: "From early on in my adolescence I seemed to have set myself a sort of task. I was trying to want only what happened, and to part with things without regret. It made me sort of on equal terms with death—I realised that it did not exist. I felt I had begun to participate in the inevitable. I knew then what bliss was. I started to live in a marvellous parenthesis" (*LV,* 248). To appreciate Constance's effort to "participate in the inevitable," the "marvellous parenthesis," it is useful for us to consider Durrell's own perspective, expressed in *A Smile in the Mind's Eye,* which was published in 1980, and the relationship of his vision to the Tao. According to the mystical philosophy of Lao-tzu, the sixth-century B.C. Chinese thinker to whom Durrell often makes reference in his letters as well as in his short memoir, the Tao is the creative principle that orders the universe. From Durrell's Taoist-influenced perspective, Constance's presence appears to be an absolutely essential balance to the joined horrors of Livia's defection, World War II, and the Gnostics' dark vision. *Livia* nudges the reader toward a similarly inclusive and balanced perspective in its evolving portrait of the Egyptian prince Hassad. The mere appellation used, "the Prince," causes the reader to associate him with the Gnostic Prince of Darkness in *Monsieur,* as do his initial willingness to help finance Hitler's program and his libertine demands at Riquiqui's house (*LV,* 148–49). The later accounts of his tender relationship with his wife Princess Fawzia and his struggles against impotence, however, lead the reader toward a more charitable understanding of his efforts to recapture the innocence and tenderness of his youthful romance and marriage even in his most libertine acts. The reader may have to stretch his moral categories to take in the Prince's full character, an exercise Taoists or Jungians would support.

In his memoir, Durrell embraces the Taoist proposition (apparently recalled from his childhood in India) that "the world [is] a Paradise, and one [is] under an obligation to realize it as fully as possible before being forced to quit it." Balancing Gnosticism, Constance's bliss of the marvellous parenthesis seems to comprehend "this galloping continuum—the natural force of the cosmos" that Durrell calls the Tao.[13] In *Livia* Blanford has only begun to recollect Constance, who will move to center stage in the novel bearing her name and remain a stay of his consciousness through the concluding two volumes.

If we draw on Durrell's brief memoir, then, to interpret the *Quintet,* the treasure Blanford will discover through his five volumes of fictive projections and ruthlessly thorough reclamations seems very much like the Tao. As such, it is the grandest psychological and philosophical reward imaginable. From the Taoist perspective, according to which man is a microcosm corresponding minutely to the macrocosm, Blanford's ultimate vision resembles what Durrell says Friedrich Nietzsche sought in his theory of eternal recurrence: "An eternal simultaneity—the continuous eternal and simultaneous presence of everything mortal or material or in essence, wrapped into a package with all Time included in it—and the whole of it present in every thought, in every drawn breath, an incandescent Now!" This simultaneity, in which "all

13. Lawrence Durrell, *A Smile in the Mind's Eye* (London, 1980), 1, 8, 36.

the temporal selves" would be "focused together now in an instant of perfect attention, of crystal-clear apprehension which could last forever," appears to be "the collective image of the past" that troubles Piers in his Gnostic investigations (*Mr,* 10). When this sought-after moment occurs, Blanford, in contrast to the Gnostics, will feel the way he does in the last sentence of the *Quintet* as "reality prime rushed to the aid of fiction and the totally unpredictable began to take place!" He will have reached "a state of total *disponibilité,* total availability, a total and comprehensive and wholehearted awareness of that instant where certainty breaks surface like a hooked fish." When that happens, "reality is then prime, independent of the hampering conceptual apparatus of conscious thought," for his mind has joined "itself to the nature of all created things."[14]

He will have used projections of inward states to refund his friends and inventions as actors who make "up one whole single personality."[15] As he discovers through the five volumes, "we exist in five-skanda form, aggregates, parcels, lots, congeries," and these "cohere to form a human being . . . and create the old force-field, quinx, the five-sided being with two arms, two legs and the kundalini as properties!" Through proper mirroring and caring, Blanford has worked through his "blissful amnesia" about the past to discover "the five-sided truth about human personality" hidden there.[16] Durrell's postmodern method here turns the novel and the central characters "deliberately . . . inside out like a sleeve . . . then back."[17] Thus becoming quinx,

14. *Ibid.,* 48; Durrell, *Quinx,* 201; Durrell, *Smile in the Mind's Eye,* 1.

15. Durrell, *Quinx,* 11.

16. *Ibid.,* 15–16. *Skandha* is Sanskrit for "aggregates"; in Buddhism the word signifies the five elements that sum up the whole of an individual's mental and physical existence: body (matter); sensations (feelings); perception of sense objects; mental formations; and reflexive awareness of the other three mental aggregates. Durrell's spelling alludes also to Skanda (Sanskrit for "spurt of semen"), Hindu god of war, the first-born son of Shiva and in some accounts of Parvati, or, in others, of fire. Skanda had six faces with which to drink the milk of his six nurses, perhaps the Pleiades; he never married and so in Yoga (often mounted on his very phallic peacock) represents the power of chastity.

17. Durrell, *Sebastian,* 124. The method here is the reverse of the more familiar modernist approach of the *Quartet,* which gives multiple perspectives of specific characters like Justine as seen by other characters. Ultimately, however, the *Quartet,* too, turns Darley himself inside out through the individuals (Justine, Mountolive, Arnauti, Pursewarden, Nessim, Narouz, and others) he "invents" out of his innermost needs and fears. Durrell's postmodern technique in the *Quintet* has since been employed to good effect

Blanford has opened himself to the rush of "reality prime" that makes the creative act inevitable. He has claimed the uncommon gold re-funded through self-exhausting imaginative projections, a discovery that leads his readers toward the philosopher's stone of our time.

---

by Philip Roth in *The Counterlife,* first published in 1986, where Nathan Zuckerman is similarly turned inside out through his fictions and selfobjects. Zuckerman, however, considers what he does a series of performances or impersonations, not a process of self-discovery or reclamation; his interpretation here may be another psychological defense. See Philip Roth, *The Counterlife* (New York, 1988), 239, 366.

CONCLUSION

Narcissus Ascending

The eleven novels selected for this study span three decades, from 1956 to 1985. In the broadest sense, during that period the six authors of those novels effected no radical change in the need for, and limit placed on, the range of character mutability. By 1959, Bellow's two novels had both raised the possibility of significant character transformations and then set a firm limit to the scope of those transformations. The earlier of the two books, *Seize the Day,* foregrounds the limit, while implying the need to change, and the later one, *Henderson the Rain King,* highlights the transformation, while implying, through its drama, the boundary of the changes possible.

However, in more subtle nuances of transformation, the six novelists progressed models of character development in essential ways. On the one hand, the satirical parodies by Pynchon and Kosinski portray the hazards of external, Protean change with a vividness that may puzzle readers but that they cannot ignore. On the other, the novels by Fowles and Barth demonstrate methods of character transformation. Although both of these latter novelists represent changes that arise from the characters' inward resources, the methods they portray differ. Whereas Barth's tales focus on the necessity of exhausting roles favored by dominant cultures in order to liberate archetypes such cultures traditionally ignore, Fowles, accepting the poverty of Nicholas' existential mask, puts his major character through an intricate maze constructed to mirror both the masculine and feminine energies Nicholas' earlier role-playing denied.

Within the limits of a single novel, *The Magus* provides as rich a map of the inner world as one will find in contemporary fiction, though Doris Lessing's brilliant *Briefing for a Descent into Hell,* published in 1971, extends that map far into the realm of madness. Compared to *The Magus,* Durrell's new series, *The Avignon Quintet,* enjoys the advantage that five volumes and roughly twice as many pages offer to employ multiple frames. Added freedom allows Durrell to represent a variety of images of negative Proteanism, especially through Mnemidis in *Sebastian,* and gives him space to represent the inward resources of Aubrey Blanford and Constance with a fullness that moves the series beyond psychological discovery into a philosophical realm embodying Durrell's personal form of Taoism.

Through his less restrained explorations, Durrell makes full use of a fundamental concept of modern psychological theory, the transference. For him, however, the transference is but a scientific reformulation of an elemental literary device, the habit of telling the inner story in terms of the outer one, an end that writers achieve (at least since Homer used the deities as a psychomechanism) by turning their characters inside out. For Durrell, the psychological and literary device called the transference amounts to the true philosopher's stone. By presenting the potential chaos of the inner life outwardly so that we can begin to understand its workings and draw on its resources rather than be driven by them, the modern stone helps transmute the dross of psychological confusion into the uncommon gold of self-knowledge.

By light reflected from this new philosopher's stone, we learn that Narcissus is the hidden name of Everyman who chooses to avoid the blinding fate of Oedipus, possibly even the dogged repetitions of Sisyphus. For the Sphinx who rules our fate is not a creature in the outer world; our Sphinx dwells within, as Oedipus' ultimately did. It is wise, therefore, to take our clue from Narcissus, not Oedipus. Indeed, we may be able to go Narcissus one better. Building on discoveries of Freud, Jung, Kohut, and the novelists discussed here, we may coax the Sphinx of our hidden selves from the waters of the unconscious rather than, like Melville's Narcissus or Oedipus or Proteus, leap after the image or images we see in the outer world.

Avoiding the fate of the ancient prototypes requires, these contemporary novelists suggest, that we transvaluate the myths of Proteus and Narcissus. This is no simple change to make. In literature for at least a century (since the demise of romanticism and the emergence of realism), external forces, or the environment, have dominated characters. (The philosophical and scientific roots of the ascendency of the objective realm are, of course, much older.) The external world is the realm from which Proteus takes his clues, the way Chance passively mirrors the television screens.

Narcissus, too, uses the outer world but chiefly as a mirror of the self and, in contemporary fiction, as a mirror of an otherwise hidden, inward self. More than Proteus, Narcissus, for a variety of reasons, bears the onus of an unfavorable reputation. In our age, Freud associated Narcissus with pathological behavior, but Freud here, Kohut reminds us, simply echoes a much older, moralized, often puritanic culture that in its innocence confuses the centered self with self-centeredness and self with selfishness. The new dispensation, coming chiefly from Kohut, indicates the opposite: that neediness of various kinds, as represented by characters as diverse as Nicholas and Henderson, Livia and Anteia, often flows from the want of a strong and centered self.[1] This new perspective forces us, therefore, to revise the popular view of Narcissus.

In recent decades, the major popularizer of narcissistic themes, Christopher Lasch, has followed the moralizing tradition. In his bestselling *The Culture of Narcissism,* he identifies modern American culture with an "ethic of self-preservation and psychic survival," "the cult of personal relations," "the cult of sensuality," and "the ideology of personal growth." American culture, he says, is a culture that, though "superficially optimistic, radiates a profound despair and resignation," for "it is the faith of those without faith." To replace this false cult(ure), he proposes a return to the "moral discipline formerly associated with the work ethic" and to "the will to build a better society" by drawing on surviving "traditions of localism, self-help, and community action that only need the vision of a new society, a decent society, to give them new vigor."[2]

In effect, Lasch has turned the concept of narcissism into a tool to be used by social critics. His list of the ills of contemporary society is a long one. He speaks of pathological characteristics: a "dependence on the vicarious warmth provided by others," as well as "a fear of dependence, a sense of inner emptiness, boundless repressed rage, and unsatisfied oral cravings." To such pathological indications he adds a

1. *Cf.* James F. Masterson's discussion of Thomas Wolfe in *The Real Self: A Developmental, Self, and Object Relations Approach* (New York, 1985), 115–66.

2. Lasch, *Culture of Narcissism,* 103, 396–97.

group of secondary characteristics: "pseudo self-insight, calculating seductiveness, nervous, self-deprecatory humor." He speaks ultimately of large patterns that mark contemporary culture, of traits such as "the intense fear of old age and death, altered sense of time, fascination with celebrity, fear of competition, decline of the play spirit, deteriorating relations between men and women"—traits that sometimes show up in the characters discussed here.[3]

From Kohut's new, less moralizing, more empathic perspective, it appears that social critics inspired by Freud's early essay on narcissism have done very nearly what Lasch proposed not to do. At the subtle level anticipated by Freud, they have equated "narcissism with everything selfish and disagreeable" in contemporary culture. Although there can be no doubt that problems associated with extreme narcissistic deprivation can lead to psychoses and borderline states (*HDAC,* 8–9, 53), narcissistic needs remain lifelong with every man and woman (*HDAC,* 61). The social critics who follow Freud in the Cartesian tradition have failed to notice how intimately narcissism is intertwined with all human perception. They have failed to honor what Lasch calls "the state of mind in which the world appears as a mirror of the self" and have dismissed this state as a metaphor.[4]

Kohut shows that the narcissistic relationship to the world is more than a metaphor. His position resembles Herman Melville's more than it does Lasch's. Melville was not using Narcissus as a mere metaphor when he called the myth of Narcissus "the key to it all," then brilliantly dramatized the Platonizing romantic desire to take nature, "the mystic ocean at [Ishmael's feet,] for the visible image of that deep, blue, bottomless soul, pervading mankind and nature." When Melville's Ahab sees in the whale, his special part of nature, an "outrageous strength, with an inscrutable malice sinewing it," or when Ahab at last comes to transfer to that whale "not only all his bodily woes, but all his intellectual and spiritual exasperations . . . all truth with malice in it . . . all the subtle demonisms of life and thought; all evil," it is not a metaphor but Melville's way of revealing Ahab's paranoid inner being.[5]

Nor is it a metaphor Kohut has in mind when he replaces the pure

3. *Ibid.,* 74–75.

4. *Ibid.,* 73, 75.

5. Melville, *Moby-Dick,* 24, 136, 139, 154.

transcendental consciousness of Husserl, the Dasein of Heidegger, Sartre's Being-for-itself, with the special relationship between a perceiver and a perceived object that Kohut terms the selfobject. The concept selfobject signifies that in our essential relationships, with individuals who mirror our worth or whom we idealize, what we perceive may belong as much to us, the subject, as to the other person, the object of our perception (*AS,* xiv; *HDAC,* 49). In some fields, objective perceptions, or Husserl's pure consciousness, if possible, would be useful. In relationships between people, however, as Fowles demonstrates throughout *The Magus,* such totally objective knowledge is improbable and not altogether desirable. In Jungian analytical psychology, much as in Kohut's self psychology, self-knowledge begins with the self coloring the world it perceives: "All unconscious contents," Jungians say, are "first experienced in *projection.*" That is, "an unconscious quality of one's own is first recognized and reacted to when it is discovered in an outer object."[6] If self-knowledge, individual growth, and joyful interactions all begin as a blurring of the line between self and objects, then it is well to be cautious about following Freud, Lasch, and others in their disparaging view of narcissistic behavior.

While building toward an empathic view of the narcissistic style, one parallel to Kohut's, the works considered here, at the same time, question in one way or another the premises of existentialism. This critique they accomplish by playing Husserl's phenomenology, on which modern existential philosophy rests, off against an empathic perspective grounded in the psychoanalytic view of human character.

Differences between the two perspectives have not always been clear to literary critics, nor are they always clear to psychoanalytical theorists. In the early days of existential writing in America, it was commonplace to assimilate existential novelists such as John Updike and Norman Mailer, even Bellow and Pynchon, to the modernist writing that dominated the first half of the century. This accommodation may have arisen because Updike, Mailer, Bellow, and writers like them employ the techniques for exploring the mind developed by the great modernist novelists, Proust, Joyce, Faulkner, and their contemporaries. As a corollary, because the Freudian view of man was a mainstay

6. Edinger, "Outline of Analytical Psychology," 4.

of such modernist thought and literature, a natural tendency existed to ignore differences between the emerging existential view of human nature and the established psychological perspective.

Efforts to accommodate psychoanalysis and existentialism within a single outlook have been numerous and have often proved fruitful. For example, as mentioned earlier, by 1970, the assimilating process was powerful enough to launch the *Journal of Phenomenological Psychology*. In the initial issue, the editorial announcing the journal's aims and policy was necessarily vague and general: "[The journal] is dedicated to the aim of approaching psychology in such a way that the entire range of experience and behavior of man as a human person may be properly studied. . . . The term 'phenomenological' is meant in the broadest sense possible, referring to the movement as a whole, and it is not intended to convey the thought of any single person." Establishment of a "constructive alternative to natural scientific psychology" appears to have been the major intent of the journal.[7]

Following a parallel impulse, the *American Journal of Psychiatry* in 1984 carried a straightforward article by psychiatrist Alfred Margulies arguing that "Husserl's phenomenological reduction and Freud's basic rule of free association bear striking affinities" to John Keats's concept of "negative capability" and therefore to one another in that all employ "a process of not-concluding . . . of keeping the mind open to new possibilities."[8] Margulies wisely restricts his case to epistemological similarities between psychoanalysis and phenomenology and avoids completely the more difficult and important ontological implications of his synthesis.[9] His omission here, though, can easily mislead theorists eager to span the gap between the two perspectives.

The result of blurring ontological differences between Freudian thought and phenomenology becomes more blatant in the work of Jacques Lacan. Currently one of the most imitated thinkers in Western intellectual circles, Lacan may have been the theorist who made most effective use of wedding Freudian psychology to modern French thought. Like Margulies, his explicit loyalty is to the science of the

7. "Editorial," *Journal of Phenomenological Psychology,* I (Fall, 1970), 5.

8. Alfred Margulies, "Toward Empathy: The Uses of Wonder," *American Journal of Psychiatry,* CXLI (1984), 1025.

9. *Cf.* Keith M. May, *Out of the Maelstrom: Psychology and the Novel in the Twentieth Century* (New York, 1977), 80–86.

psyche. When we look beneath the surface, however, we discover Lacan's deeper loyalty lies with the phenomenological philosophy coming out of Husserl by way of Heidegger and Sartre.[10]

The implications of Lacan's covert commitment to phenomenology should be clear to readers who know the basic assumptions of Freud and Husserl. The way in which Lacan's position runs counter to Freud has, for example, become a recent concern of psychoanalytic and reader-response critic Norman N. Holland. In a forthcoming essay, Holland argues that Lacan "turns psychoanalysis into philosophy (or choplogic)," that "he thinks in logical either-ors that generate paradoxes and false dichotomies (such as self *or* language)," whereas "true psychoanalytic thought," Holland writes, deals with "both-and" ways of thinking. He points out that the Saussurean linguistics on which Lacan builds his argument is not only discredited by contemporary linguistics but "a fundamentally anti-psychoanalytic, stimulus-response model of a self-running language." Ferdinand de Saussure, according to Holland, "asserts (in the language of reader-response criticism) a text-active model, an account of language devoid of persons, that Lacan pushes even further," to the point of dropping "the self out of, not just language, but all psychic functioning, not because of evidence or logic, but Saussure's discredited linguistics."[11]

Holland's perception that the assumptions underlying Lacan's theory assault the self expresses the sense created by all the novels discussed in the present study. Whereas Holland uses Noam Chomsky's structural theory of linguistics to frame the approach of Saussure and Lacan, the novelists represented here implicitly generate a language theory of their own. For Saussure and Lacan, a language is a system of imperfect signs. For Chomsky, it is a pattern of self-generating forms relatively free of semantic content. Our six novelists, in contrast, imply that beyond its structural and signifying elements, a language is finally

10. Anthony Wilden, "Lacan and the Discourse of the Other," in Jacques Lacan, *The Language of the Self: The Function of Language in Psychoanalysis,* trans. Anthony Wilden (Baltimore, 1968), 160; John P. Muller and William J. Richardson, *Lacan and Language: A Reader's Guide to "Ecrits"* (New York, 1982), 22.

11. Norman N. Holland, "I-ing Lacan," in *Criticism and Lacan: Essays and Dialogue on Language, Structure, and the Unconscious,* ed. Patrick Colm Hogan, in *IPSA Abstracts and Bibliography in Literature and Psychology,* IV (May, 1989), 7. See also Norman N. Holland, "The Trouble(s) with Lacan," unpublished essay, available from *IPSA,* University of Florida, Gainesville, 1990.

a pattern of mirrors. For example, as the word *intimacy* often mirrors behaviors and emotions in the psyche of a woman that differ remarkably from those it mirrors in a man's imagination, or the word *God* means radically different things to a Greek and to a Jew, or to a Moslem and to a Hindu, the word *love* to the pursuer and the pursued, so the name *Alison* reflects (and thus means) an emotional reality in Nicholas' psyche at the end of *The Magus* that differs profoundly from what that same name mirrored at the start. In a similar fashion, each novel in turn initially finds the reader in a relatively familiar time and place, then leads him through a maze of mirroring words that to varying degrees reflect less familiar materials of the reader's inner world, and, by so doing, the novel causes an alchemy to transpire in the reader like the psychic transformations that Henderson, Nicholas, Perseus, Blanford, and Constance undergo. As a group, the novels carry us from the familiar urban world of Tommy Wilhelm, with his choked-up need to change, through the hazardous choices that Herbert Stencil, Nicholas, and Chance confront, to the fecund "reality prime" that tugs Blanford as *Quinx* comes to a close.

The eleven novels, however, respond not to Lacan's theory of signs but to the ontology that underlies Lacan's position. Although Holland does not stress it, Lacan's rejection of the self in favor of language, the phenomenon through which Lacan claims we construct the "subject that desires," is a clear echo of the phenomenological tradition that dominated French intellectual life during the middle third of the twentieth century. (On modern French intellectual life, Durrell, in *Sebastian,* has Vienna-trained Constance think of homicidal Mnemidis: "In murder he perfected himself, you might say! An existentialist formulation worthy of the Left Bank!" She goes on to describe the Left Bank as the "Babel . . . being built by Sartre and Lacan and their followers, swarming like flies on the eyeballs of a dying horse!") From the phenomenological perspective, the self and the unconscious remain theoretical fictions. Husserl's transcendental ego, however, immediately experiences the language that "constitutes" the Cartesian "subject that desires to be."[12]

In contrast to the Cartesian ideal that Husserl's followers pursue, these eleven novels either dramatize the risks of phenomenological ap-

12. Wilden, "Lacan and the Discourse of the Other," 160; Durrell, *Sebastian,* 102; Muller and Richardson, *Lacan and Language,* 19–23.

proaches to character or, in strong opposition to the theory of being derived from Husserl, establish the biological and psychological roots of personality that phenomenologists prefer to bracket and thus leave at the periphery of consciousness. For reasons given in this study, the effects of blurring differences between the philosophical and psychoanalytic models of character, or of choosing one model over the other, are a good deal more significant than Margulies or Lacan acknowledge.

There is a sense, however, in which the two models converge in the figure of Narcissus himself, as described by Kohut. If we accept Kohut's interpretation of modernist art's use of fragments (*RS,* 286–88), Proteus may be another name for Narcissus as he appears in the fragmented figures of Eliot's *Waste Land,* Pound's *Cantos,* and cubist paintings. Proteus is also the name Narcissus assumes in the fiction of existentialism when he grandiosely seeks the abstract, transcendent freedom of change without limits. To Kohut, Proteus would be the fragmented or grandiose form of Narcissus. But Narcissus becomes our contemporary hero's name when he faces the self in the mirror, accepts practical limits, and struggles to center in a solid self.

Because Narcissus, from Kohut's perspective, subsumes the psychoanalytic and phenomenological models, he appears as the central figure in contemporary Western culture. He is the face in the mirror of our private rooms as well as of our semipublic art. As such, he is too important to be judged and dismissed the way Lasch does.

In our age, Kohut initiated the defense of Narcissus. More recently, Anthony Storr, in *Solitude: A Return to the Self,* published in 1988, has reminded us how intimately the centered self is bound up with the creative act. At the same time, Stephen M. Johnson has continued the process of "humanizing" the narcissistic style that Bellow began with Henderson, Pynchon with Fausto, Fowles with Nicholas, Kosinski with his minor characters, Barth with Perseus, and Durrell with Blanford and Tu.

All the books discussed here are brilliant novels, especially in their thematic visions, even though their methods differ. The aesthetics underlying the eleven novels vary so greatly that attempting to evaluate the books relative to one another would be like comparing apples and oranges. On the one hand, *Seize the Day* is an almost perfect late-modernist novel: short and carefully constructed as to point of view, imagery, texture, tone, unity of setting, action, character. On the other hand, *The Avignon Quintet* participates in the still-emerging aesthetic of postmodern fiction; its many pages contain great shifts in setting, characters, action, tone, texture, and point of view. In between these two works fall the relative looseness of transitional novels such as *Henderson, The Magus,* and *Being There* and the relative tightness of *V.,* another transitional work, and of *Chimera,* a fully postmodern work.[13] What the six novelists share is a conceptual brilliance. They are not merely describing manners, conditions, and actions; they are creating a new vision of the possibilities and limits that define human behavior.

Having said a good deal about Proteus and Narcissus, I have to acknowledge that resolution of the struggle for intellectual hegemony between phenomenology and psychoanalysis ultimately lies well beyond the scope of this study. I can only report on forms the conflict takes in an important group of contemporary novels. For reasons documented here, the debate between the two perspectives may be the most lively and important struggle in the postmodern intellectual arena. Our focus has, of necessity, been limited to a group of brilliant novelists who, having understood what the phenomenological point of view implies, chose to dramatize its dangers and alternatives rather than embrace it enthusiastically the way midcentury thinkers and artists did.[14] In part because they resist the pull of Proteus, in part because they accept the Narcissus in each of us, in part because they discover brilliant forms that liberate the force of Narcissus, they continue to serve English and American readers as the advance guard of the postmodern movement.

13. I am now writing a study of the transition Durrell and Fowles made from the modernist aesthetic to the postmodern.

14. Among the novelists one might include Richard Wright, Norman Mailer, the early John Updike, and William Styron; *cf.* May, *Out of the Maelstrom,* 90–97.

BIBLIOGRAPHY

Adler, Alfred. *The Individual Psychology of Alfred Adler.* Edited by Heinz L. Ansbacher and Rowena R. Ansbacher. New York, 1956.

———. *The Science of Living.* Edited by Heinz L. Ansbacher. Garden City, N.Y., 1969.

Aharoni, Ada. "Bellow and Existentialism." *Saul Bellow Journal,* II (1983), 42–54.

Alter, Robert. "The Stature of Saul Bellow." *Midstream,* X (December, 1964), 3–15.

Barnes, Julian. "Trick or Treat." *New Statesman,* September 22, 1978, pp. 377–78.

Barth, John. *Chimera.* New York, 1972.

———. *The End of the Road.* New York, 1969.

———. *The Floating Opera.* New York, 1956.

———. *Lost in the Funhouse.* Garden City, N.Y., 1968.

———. *The Sot-Weed Factor.* New York, 1964.

Bellow, Saul. *Henderson the Rain King.* In *The Portable Saul Bellow.* New York, 1974.

———. *Seize the Day.* New York, 1961.

———. "Where Do We Go from Here: The Future of Fiction." In *The Theory of the American Novel,* edited by George Perkins. New York, 1970.

Berger, Gaston. *The "Cogito" in Husserl's Philosophy.* Translated by Kathleen McLaughlin. Evanston, Ill., 1972.

Berman, Morris. *The Reenchantment of the World.* New York, 1984.

Bettelheim, Bruno. "The Problem of Generations." In *The Challenge of Youth,* edited by Erik H. Erikson. Garden City, N.Y., 1965.

Bienstock, Beverly Gray. "Lingering on the Autognostic Verge: John Barth's *Lost in the Funhouse.*" *Modern Fiction Studies,* XIX (Spring, 1973), 69–78.

Brock, Werner. "An Account of 'Being and Time.'" In *Existence and Being,* by Martin Heidegger. Chicago, 1949.

Campbell, Joseph. *The Hero with a Thousand Faces.* Princeton, 1972.

Carley, James P. "Lawrence Durrell's Avignon Quincunx and Gnostic Heresy." *Malahat Review,* LXI (1982), 156–67.

Cirlot, J. E. *A Dictionary of Symbols.* New York, 1962.

Clayton, John. *Saul Bellow: In Defense of Man.* Bloomington, 1968.

Dodds, E. R. *The Greeks and the Irrational.* Berkeley, 1968.

Durrell, Lawrence. *Constance, or Solitary Practices.* New York, 1982.

———. *An Irish Faustus: A Morality in Nine Scenes.* New York, 1964.

———. *Livia, or Buried Alive*. New York, 1984.
———. *Monsieur.* New York, 1984.
———. *Quinx, or The Ripper's Tale*. New York, 1986.
———. *Sebastian, or Ruling Passions*. New York, 1984.
———. *A Smile in the Mind's Eye*. London. 1980.
Edie, James M. *Edmund Husserl's Phenomenology.* Bloomington, 1987.
———. "Introduction." In *The "Cogito" in Husserl's Philosophy,* by Gaston Berger. Evanston, Ill., 1972.
Edinger, Edward F. "An Outline of Analytical Psychology." *Quadrant,* I (1968). Rpr.
"Editorial." *Journal of Phenomenological Psychology,* I (Fall, 1970), 5.
Enright, D. J. "Great Slow Verbs." *Listener,* October 17, 1974, p. 513.
Fowles, John. "Hardy and the Hag." In *Thomas Hardy After Fifty Years,* edited by Lance St. John Butler. Totowa, N.J., 1977.
———. *The Magus*. Boston, 1965.
———. *The Magus: A Revised Version*. Boston, 1977.
———, to Julius Rowan Raper, January 8, 1989.
Franz, M.-L. von. "The Process of Individuation." In *Man and His Symbols,* edited by Carl G. Jung. Garden City, N.Y., 1970.
Frazer, James G. *The Golden Bough*. New York, 1951.
Freud, Sigmund. *Beyond the Pleasure Principle*. Translated by James Strachey. New York, 1959.
———. *Civilization and Its Discontents*. Edited and translated by James Strachey. New York, 1961.
———. "Contributions to the Psychology of Love: The Most Prevalent Form of Degradation in Erotic Life." In Vol. IV of Freud, *Collected Papers,* translated by Joan Riviere. London, 1934. 4 vols.
———. "On Narcissism: An Introduction." In Vol. IV of Freud, *Collected Papers,* edited by Joan Riviere. London, 1934. 4 vols.
———. "Repression." In *A General Selection from the Works of Sigmund Freud,* edited by John Rickman. Garden City, N.Y., 1957.
Glasgow, Ellen. *The Sheltered Life*. Garden City, N.Y., 1932.
Gogol, John M. "Kosinski's Chance: McLuhan Age Narcissus." *Notes on Contemporary Literature,* I (September, 1971), 8–10.
Grunberger, Bela. *Narcissism: Psychoanalytic Essays*. Translated by Joyce S. Diamanti. New York, 1979.
Handy, William J. "Saul Bellow and the Naturalistic Hero." *Texas Studies in Literature and Language,* V (Winter, 1964), 538–45.
Harris, Charles B. *Passionate Virtuosity: The Fiction of John Barth*. Urbana, 1983.
Heidegger, Martin. *Basic Writings from "Being and Time" (1927) to "The Task of Thinking" (1964)*. Edited by David Farrell Krell. New York, 1977.

———. *Being and Time*. Translated by John Macquarrie and Edward Robinson. New York, 1962.

———. *Existence and Being*. Chicago, 1949.

Holland, Norman N. "I-ing Lacan." In *Criticism and Lacan: Essays and Dialogue on Language, Structure, and the Unconscious,* edited by Patrick Colm Hogan. In *IPSA Abstracts and Bibliography in Literature and Psychology,* IV (May, 1989), 7.

———. "The Trouble(s) with Lacan." Unpublished essay, 1990. Available from *IPSA,* University of Florida, Gainesville.

Holm, Astrid. "Existentialism and Saul Bellow's *Henderson, the Rain King*." *American Studies in Scandinavia,* X (1978), 93–109.

Huffaker, Robert. *John Fowles*. Boston, 1980.

Hunt, John W. "Comic Escape and Anti-Vision: The Novels of Joseph Heller and Thomas Pynchon." In *Adversity and Grace,* edited by Nathan A. Scott, Jr. Chicago, 1968.

Husserl, Edmund. *Logical Investigations*. Translated by J. N. Findlay. Vol. I of 2 vols. London, 1970.

Jacobsen, Thorkild. "Toward the Image of Tammuz." *History of Religion,* I (Winter, 1961), 189–213.

Johnson, Robert A. *She: Understanding Feminine Psychology*. New York, 1977.

Johnson, Stephen M. *Humanizing the Narcissistic Style*. New York, 1987.

Jung, C. G. *The Archetypes and the Collective Unconscious*. Translated by R. F. C. Hull. New York, 1959.

———. "The Meaning of Psychology for Modern Man." In *Civilization in Transition*. New York, 1964.

———. *Memories, Dreams, Reflections*. Edited by Aniela Jaffé. New York, 1965.

———. *Psyche and Symbol: A Selection from the Writings of C. G. Jung*. Edited by Violet S. de Laszlo. Garden City, N.Y., 1958.

———. *Psychological Types; or, The Psychology of Individuation*. Translated by H. Godwin Baynes. New York, 1933.

———. *Two Essays on Analytical Psychology*. Translated by R. F. C. Hull. New York, 1956.

———, *et al. Man and His Symbols*. Garden City, N.Y., 1964.

Kockelmans, Joseph J. "Husserl's Original View on Phenomenological Psychology." In *Phenomenological Psychology: The Dutch School,* edited by Joseph J. Kockelmans. Dordrecht, The Netherlands, 1987.

Kohut, Heinz. *The Analysis of the Self*. New York, 1971.

———. *How Does Analysis Cure?* Edited by Arnold Goldberg. Chicago, 1984.

———. *The Restoration of the Self*. New York, 1977.

———. *Self Psychology and the Humanities*. Edited by Charles B. Strozier. New York, 1985.

———, and Ernest S. Wolf. "The Disorders of the Self and Their Treatment: An Outline." *International Journal of Psycho-Analysis,* LIX (1978), 413–25.

Kosinski, Jerzy. *Being There*. New York, 1970.

Lacan, Jacques. *The Language of the Self: The Function of Language in Psychoanalysis*. Translated by Anthony Wilden. Baltimore, 1968.

Lasch, Christopher. *The Culture of Narcissism: American Life in an Age of Diminishing Expectations*. New York, 1979.

Lavers, Norman. *Jerzy Kosinski*. Boston, 1982.

Levenson, Michael H. *A Genealogy of Modernism: A Study of English Literary Doctrine 1908–1922*. Cambridge, Eng., 1986.

Lévy-Bruhl, Lucien. *Primitive Mentality*. London, 1923.

Lifton, Robert Jay. *Boundaries: Psychological Man in Revolution*. New York, 1970.

MacNiven, Ian S., and Harry T. Moore, eds. *Literary Lifelines: The Richard Aldington—Lawrence Durrell Correspondence*. New York, 1981.

Malcolm, Henry. *Generation of Narcissus*. Boston, 1971.

Margulies, Alfred. "Toward Empathy: The Uses of Wonder." *American Journal of Psychiatry,* CXLI (1984), 1025–33.

Masterson, James F. *The Real Self: A Developmental, Self, and Object Relations Approach*. New York, 1985.

May, Keith M. *Out of the Maelstrom: Psychology and the Novel in the Twentieth Century*. New York, 1977.

McNeill, William H. *The Rise of the West: A History of the Human Community*. New York, 1963.

Melville, Herman. *Moby-Dick; or, The Whale*. Edited by Alfred Kazin. Boston, 1956.

Morrell, David. *John Barth: An Introduction*. University Park, Pa., 1976.

Moss, Robert F. "*Monsieur* by Lawrence Durrell." *New Republic,* February 22, 1975, p. 30.

Muller, John P., and William J. Richardson. *Lacan and Language: A Reader's Guide to "Ecrits."* New York, 1982.

Mulvey, Christopher E. Review of *The Magus,* by John Fowles. *Commonweal,* April 1, 1966, pp. 60–61.

Nilson, Helge Normann. "Saul Bellow and Wilhelm Reich." *American Studies in Scandinavia,* X (1978), 81–91.

Olshen, Barry N. "John Fowles's *The Magus:* An Allegory of Self-Realization." *Journal of Popular Culture,* IX (Spring, 1976), 916–25.

Perls, Frederick, Ralph E. Hefferline, and Paul Goodman. *Gestalt Therapy: Excitement and Growth in the Human Personality*. New York, 1951.

Polster, Erving, and Miriam Polster. *Gestalt Therapy Integrated: Contours of Theory and Practice*. New York, 1973.

Porter, M. Gilbert. *Whence the Power? The Artistry and Humanity of Saul Bellow.* Columbia, Mo., 1974.

Pribanic, Victor. "The Monomyth and its Function in *Henderson the Rain King.*" In *Itinerary 3: Criticism,* edited by Frank Baldanza. Bowling Green, Ohio, 1977.

Pynchon, Thomas. *V.* New York, 1986.

Review of *V.,* by Thomas Pynchon. *Commentary,* XXXVI (Spring, 1963), 258.

Richey, Clarence W. "'Being There' and *Dasein:* A Note on the Philosophical Presupposition Underlying the Novels of Jerzy Kosinski." *Notes on Contemporary Literature,* II (September, 1972), 13–15.

Robbe-Grillet, Alain. *For a New Novel: Essays on Fiction.* Translated by Richard Howard. New York, 1965.

Rodrigues, Eusebio L. "Reichianism in *Henderson the Rain King.*" *Criticism,* XV (1973), 212–33.

Roth, Philip. *The Counterlife.* New York, 1988.

Sartre, Jean-Paul. *Being and Nothingness: An Essay on Phenomenological Ontology.* New York, 1956.

———. *The Transcendence of the Ego: An Existentialist Theory of Consciousness.* Translated by Forrest Williams and Robert Kirkpatrick. New York, 1957.

Shaffer, Cheryle Lamberth. "Maternal Relationships in the Early Novels of John Fowles." M.A. thesis, University of North Carolina, 1989.

Simon, Bennett. *Mind and Madness in Ancient Greece: The Classical Roots of Modern Psychiatry.* Ithaca, 1980.

Skow, John. Review of *Monsieur,* by Lawrence Durrell. *Time,* January 27, 1975, pp. 79–80.

Slater, Philip E. *The Glory of Hera: Greek Mythology and the Greek Family.* Boston, 1968.

Slatoff, Walter. Review of *V.,* by Thomas Pynchon. *Epoch,* XII (Spring, 1963), 255–57.

Sohn, David. "A Nation of Videots." *Media and Methods,* XI (April, 1975), 24–31, 52–57.

Stein, Murray, ed. *Jungian Analysis.* Boulder, 1984.

Storr, Anthony. *Solitude: A Return to the Self.* New York, 1988.

Thwaite, Anthony. Review of *Livia,* by Lawrence Durrell. *Observer* (London), September 17, 1978, p. 34.

Trowbridge, Clinton W. "Water Imagery in *Seize the Day.*" *Critique: Studies in Modern Fiction,* IX (1966–67), 62–73.

Ulanov, Ann Bedford. "Transference/Countertransference: A Jungian Perspective." In *Jungian Analysis,* edited by Murray Stein. Boulder, 1984.

Vermeule, Emily. *Greece in the Bronze Age.* Chicago, 1972.

Wallerstein, Robert S. "Self Psychology and 'Classical' Psychoanalytical Psychology: The Nature of Their Relationship." In *The Future of Psychoanalysis,* edited by Arnold Goldberg. New York, 1983.

Webb, Constance. *Richard Wright: A Biography.* New York, 1968.

Weiss, Daniel. "Caliban on Prospero: A Psychoanalytic Study on the Novel *Seize the Day,* by Saul Bellow." In *Saul Bellow and the Critics,* edited by Irving Malin. New York, 1967.

Wickes, George, ed. *Lawrence Durrell and Henry Miller: A Private Correspondence.* New York, 1963.

Wilden, Anthony. "Lacan and the Discourse of the Other." In Jacques Lacan, *The Language of the Self: The Function of Language in Psychoanalysis,* trans. Anthony Wilden. Baltimore, 1968.

Winchell, Mark Roydon. "Bellow's Hero with a Thousand Faces: The Use of Folk Myth in *Henderson the Rain King.*" *Mississippi Folklore Register,* XIV (1980), 115–26.

Winnicott, D. W. "Transitional Objects and Transitional Phenomena." In *Playing and Reality.* London, 1971.

Wolf, Ernest S. "Psychoanalytic Psychology of the Self and Literature." *New Literary History,* XII (1980), 41–60.

Worringer, Wilhelm. *Abstraction and Empathy: A Contribution to the Psychology of Style.* Translated by Michael Bullock. New York, 1953.

INDEX